Praise for *Reformational Manhood*

It is with great pleasure that I strongly recommend this insightful book, *Reformational Manhood*, from my former student and friend Greg Gibson. Greg speaks with amazing wisdom, insight and knowledge of Biblical truth for one so young. He makes his case plainly, straightforwardly and clearly. If the young men of today's church could read, digest and apply a fraction of his words of wisdom in this book, the result could be a reformation in this generation.

—JAMES PARKER, III
Professor of Worldview and Culture
The Southern Baptist Theological Seminary
Louisville, KY

We live in a culture filled with adolescent adult men who live more for entertainment than the mission of God. Greg Gibson confronts our time with a practical theology of biblical manhood. With enthusiasm for what men could be rather than merely condemning a generation for failing, Gibson challenges young men to give their lives to more than video games and pop cultural definitions of manhood. I will use this book and will recommend it often to young men I know.

—ALVIN L. REID
Professor of Evangelism and Student Ministry
Bailey Smith Chair of Evangelism
Southeastern Baptist Theological Seminary
Wake Forest, NC

Reformational Manhood is one of the most encouraging books I have read in a while. It's packed with good biblical exegesis, Christic theology, and personal testimony from a godly young man. This is a bold and uncompromising text that takes strong stances on the big and small stuff alike. It will give guidance to a generation that is crying out for leadership and investment. Buy a box of copies, study them with church members, and recommit yourself to discipling your sons and the sons of fathers who have left their boys behind. Our need is great, but our gospel is greater.

—OWEN STRACHAN
Assistant professor of Christian Theology and Church History
Boyce College
coauthor, *Essential Edwards Collection*

Reformational Manhood is a clear, helpful, and gospel-centered call to young men to embrace God's design for their lives. I've had the opportunity to know Greg for a long time now, and the principles he espouses in this book have been hammered out in the crucible of his own journey to biblical manhood. I highly recommend this resource for emerging young men (and those who work with them)."

—BRANDON SHIELDS
Lead Pastor of Soma Church
Indianapolis, IN
author of *Perspectives on Family Ministry*

REFORMATIONAL MANHOOD

Creating an Army of Gospel Centered Warriors

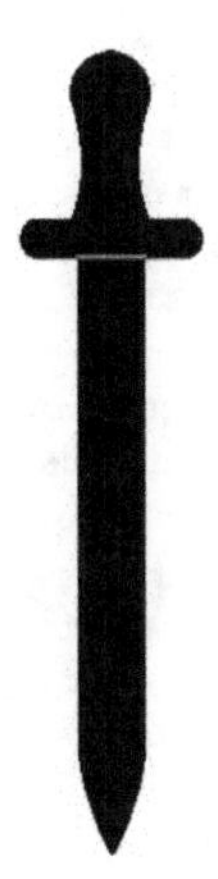

BorderStone Press, LLC
2014

Second Edition

Reformational Manhood
Creat ng an Army of
Gospel Centered Warr ors

Greg Gibson

BorderStone Press, LLC., PO Box 1383, Mountain Home, AR 72654

www.borderstonepress.com

Senior Acquisitions Editor: Roger D. Duke
Supervising editor: Brian R. Mooney

ISBN-13:978-0692544235
ISBN-10:0692544232

Contents

CONTENTS

TO GRACE

I promise you my deepest love, my fullest devotion, and strongest courage

—Preface—

†

OUR CULTURE IS teaching young boys that it's okay to be addicted to TV and video games. It's normal to see husbands portrayed as idiots in the media. It's also commonplace for boys to treat women as inferior. When we read the Bible, however, we see a completely different picture painted by our Creator.

As the church strives to accomplish the Great Commission, it is imperative that we train boys to be men. They must learn to put down boyish games and live with conviction, purpose, and endurance. They must be students of God's Word and dedicated to leading their family and the church.

When I first met Greg Gibson, he was a young seventh grade boy in love with basketball and had little concern with God's plan for his life. Over the years, I've watched him navigate through his spiritual journey and grow into a Godly man. Greg's book, *Reformational Manhood*, is a product of his journey. He has faced the challenges that all young men face in a culture saturated with sex and materialism. By sharing his struggles and applying God's Word, Greg shares tough truth that men must learn and churches must teach.

Reformational Manhood is an urgent call for young men to pursue God's plan as leaders, providers, and protectors of their families and God's church. I know you will be challenged as you read Greg's careful study of Scripture and his practical application.

I recommend this book for all men looking for answers about becoming a Godly man. I was in student ministry for eleven years before planting Foothills Church, and during that time I wish I had a book like this to take my high school guys through to challenge their spiritual growth. It's a must have for college and youth pastors. And it can also serve as a guide for fathers who want a practical approach in training their sons to grow as godly men.

If you are like me, then you have piles of really good and helpful books waiting to be read. It can be difficult to prioritize these books. I truly believe that Greg has something powerful and worthwhile to say in this book, and that this book belongs on the tops of your piles. I know that your parenting skills, as well as your personal journey, will be blessed by what you are about to read.

—DR. TRENTON J. STEWART
Church Planter, Lead Pastor, Foothills Church

—Introduction—

Why Another Book on Biblical Manhood?

LET ME BEGIN by approaching this question with fear and trepidation, for I understand that venturing into such a well-defined genre is no trivial matter. There are many weightier resources than the one before you, and ones that I would recommend before this one. Traveling into the world of John Piper, Wayne Grudem, Andreas Kostenberger, Stuart Scott, and others is, I must admit, rather scary. So, the question is begged, "Why write another book on *biblical manhood?*"

Many of the resources on biblical manhood are exhaustive and theological. The weight of their jargon makes them very heavy for the average young person, and thus many of these books fall short of reaching a broad Christian audience. I hope this book is written without so much jargon that you would put aside it after reading the first page. Nonetheless, I do want to challenge your mind and to teach you a few big words and rather complex ideas that you can add to your arsenal along the way. The other drawback of many books on manhood is that they are so fluffy or over-the-top-cheesy that I would not recommend them to anybody. They are not apt for college students or young people thinking through what the Bible says a man is supposed to be and how he is supposed to live in our culture today.

My purpose in this short and concise book is simple. It is to engage the hearts of men with relevant and thought-provoking material on what being a man—full of courage, heavy with humble leadership, standing firm on truth, etc.—actually means according to the Bible.

What a task!

The Bible never says, "This is what a man is supposed to be," but it does give us glimpses and guidelines from Genesis to Revelation about how God intends a man to live in this world as a leader, provider, and protector, as well as how a man should relate to, and treat, women.

The Holy Spirit has given me a burden for the guys who still live with their parents and play video games all day. I have had countless conversations with young guys about how they have no idea what they want to do with their life. I have seen numerous young men grow up in church and leave the church after moving out of mom and dad's house. I know hundreds of guys who are married with children and have no idea what biblical manhood is.[1] The statistics speak for themselves. George Barna says, "Many twenty-somethings are reversing course after having been active church attenders during their teenage years. As teenagers, more than half attended church each week and more than 4 out of 5 (81%) had attended a Christian church. That means that from high school graduation to age 25 there is a 42% drop in weekly church attendance and a 58% decline from ages 18 to 29. That represents about 8,000,000 twenty-somethings alive today who were active church-goers as teenagers but who will no longer be active in a church by their 30th birthday."[2]

Here are some more heavy statistics to get you started in thinking about why this topic is important:

- The typical U.S. congregation draws an adult crowd that is 61% female and 39% male. This gender gap shows up in all age categories.[3]
- On any given Sunday there are 13 million more adult women than men in America's churches.[4]
- This Sunday almost 25% of married, churchgoing women will worship without their husbands.[5]

---

[1]In a way, this book is written to all of them.

[2]George Barna, "Twentysomethings Struggle to Find Their Place in Christian Churches," *The Barna Update,* September 24, 2003, The Barna Group, www.barna.org/FlexPage.aspx?Page=BarnaUpdate&BarnaUpdateID =149.

[3]"U.S. Congregational Life Survey – Key Findings," 29 October 2003, <www.uscongregations.org/key.htm>.

[4]David Murrow, "Where Are All the Men?" <http://churchformen.com/allmen.php>.

[5]Ibid.

- Participants in midweek activities are 70% to 80% female.[6]
- The majority of church employees are women (except for ordained clergy, who are overwhelmingly male).[7]
- Over 70% of the boys being raised in church will abandon it during their teens and twenties. Many of these boys will never return.[8]
- More than 90% of American men believe in God, and five out of six call themselves Christians. But only two out of six attend church on a given Sunday. The average man accepts the reality of Jesus Christ, but fails to see any value in going to church.[9]
- Churches overseas report gender gaps of up to nine women for every adult man in attendance.[10]
- Christian universities are becoming convents. The typical Christian college in the U.S. enrolls almost two women for every man.[11]
- In a typical week, mothers are more likely than fathers to attend church, pray, read the Bible, participate in a small group, attend Sunday

---

[6]Barna Research Online, "Women are the Backbone of Christian Congregations in America," 6 March 2000, <www.barna.org>.

[7]Ibid.

[8]"LifeWay Research Uncovers Reasons 18 to 22 Year Olds Drop Out of Church," PowerPoint presentation accompanying study, available at the LifeWay Website, http://www.lifeway.com/lwc/article_main_page/0,1703,A=165949 &M=200906,00.html, accessed 12 September 2007.

[9]Barna, "Women are the Backbone of Christian Congregations in America."

[10]David Murrow, "Where Are All the Men?"

[11][9] Camerin Courtney, "O Brother, Where Art Thou?" *Christianity Today,* Single Minded. View at http://www.christianitytoday.com/singles/news letter/mind40630.html.

> school, and volunteer some of their time to help a non-profit organization.[12]

We must ask, "What has happened to all the men?" This book is my journey into what a man is supposed to be according to the Bible. It has been my experience that we often fail to teach young people what manhood is in the church. More often than not, our young people learn what manhood is supposed to be from the culture and not from their fathers or other godly men in the church. I have seen this happen over and over again. This is absolutely contradictory to Scripture, and from the statistics above, we should be ashamed of ourselves! We are losing young men every day to the attractions and influences of the culture.[13]

We are already battling against the principalities and evils of this world[14] and the world will be temporarily victorious if we sit by passively and do nothing about the next generations. Let me be clear, however, Jesus will be the ultimate victor. He has *already* defeated sin and death but has *not yet* defeated it in its entirety, as he will one day come again to completely defeat sin and death and usher in the new heavens and new earth.

---

[12]Barna Research Online, "The Spirituality of Moms Outpaces that of Dads." May 7, 2007. <http://www.barna.org/barna-update/article/15-familykids/104-the-spirituality-of-moms-outpaces-that-of-dads?q=men>

[13]Also, I am ever grateful for pastors like Mark Driscoll of Mars Hill Church in Seattle, WA, who so audaciously state they are going after the men in their city, and are in some way the leaders of this biblical manhood resurgence. I have heard him say more than once that they go after the men because when they reach the men they than reach the women. Case in point, do guys hang out in tearooms with women? Do women hangout in bars with men? Conclusion - women go where the men are; therefore, we must reach men.

[14]Ephesians 6:12.

This is one man's passionate cry to other men to begin to act like men, and to begin to train and equip young guys for manhood now! Do not hesitate! Let us begin to be men according to the standards of Jesus and not of culture. Let us humbly submit ourselves to the authority of older men who walk with God and allow them to teach us to do the same. If we do not do this then the culture will, by default, teach our up-and-coming men what manhood is.

If you are a teenager reading this book, I pray that you begin to hold a high view of biblical manhood, if you haven't already, at an early age! I pray that you would begin to apply these principles and truths to your life now, rather than delay the process of manhood until later in life. If you are a college student, then I pray you take seriously what is said in these pages. Preparing oneself to be a man is a much greater task than the pursuit of a college degree. Though both are important the former has much longer lasting benefits. Finally, if you are a man well beyond your college and teenage years and have somehow happened to venture upon this book, then I welcome you as well. Let us journey together into what a man is supposed to be according to Scripture.

I have been fleshing out and applying the principles in this book for a few years now. Much of what is written within these pages I have learned from others, whether it was on the basketball court, in the classroom, sitting at a restaurant, or simply observing *bibli-*

cal manhood in daily life (i.e., my dad, papaw, brothers, father-in-law, coaches, teachers, pastors, mentors, etc). Practicing biblical manhood comes in many different facets. It is learning how to be a leader in your home and work place. It is developing the characteristics of courage and quick decision-making. It is learning how to work hard, break a sweat, and use your time in a redemptive manner. It is loving your family and local church above everything else. And it is being a man of truth who loves Jesus and models his manhood after him, the perfect man.

I would like to thank my amazing wife, Grace, for her favor and patience through this writing process. To paraphrase Luther, when I depart from this earth, I go to the only one who loves me more than thee. I pray to be this type of man for you the rest of my days. I would also like to recognize and thank the brilliant Jonathan Riddle for spending countless hours with me working through this manuscript. I am forever thankful for your input and time brother. What's more, I would like to thank Foothills Church for allowing me to create an army of young men who are striving to practice this pursuit of biblical manhood. I would like to thank all of those who read through the drafts and encouraged me through the process of writing this book: Trent Stewart, Tyler Smith, Owen Strachan, Alvin Reid, Brandon Shields, Zack Thurman, Gabe Slone, Whitney Clayton, Ryan Rindels, and several more I wish I could list. And finally, I would like to thank Roger Duke, who approached me about two years ago to join and partner with *The Veritas Network*. Thank you for taking a chance on this young man! I would have never imagined that our relationship would have led to this book.

Please feel free to question, argue, agree, amen, and apply what you are about to read. Indeed, I urge you to. I pray that my story in this book influences you and your journey towards being a man who practices biblical manhood. Now we must ask: *What is this courageous and reformational approach to biblical manhood all about?*

"In a sort of ghastly simplicity we remove the organ and demand the function. We make men without chests and expect of them virtue and enterprise. We laugh at honour and are shocked to find traitors in our midst. We castrate and bid the geldings be fruitful." C.S. LEWIS, *The Abolition of Man,* 26

—CHAPTER ONE—

THE ABOLITION OF MANHOOD

Learning Why Men Should Not Paint Their Toenails

WHEN I WAS ELEVEN years old I had the great idea of painting my toenails red. Well, it wasn't a preconceived thought, it just happened, and I've never actually had the courage to come out in the open and confess it before![1] It actually feels kind of nice! I did tell my wife, but she just laughed out of sheer embarrassment for me.

As the story goes, I was spending the day at my grandparents' house in the country of East Tennessee. Maybe I was bored or maybe I was crazy, or a combination of the two, but I went into the bathroom and

[1] I did give this illustration in an article that I wrote for *The Veritas Network* called "Teaching Kids Proper Gender Roles". You can find the article at ***http://theveritasnetwork.org/ - Archives May 2010.***

painted my toenails red. Little did I know that it would dry and to my eleven-year-old brain there was no way to remove this polish from my toes. I tried scraping it off with a fork. I tried soap. I tried rubbing my toenails on concrete! Nothing would get this stuff off. I could only look in the mirror and feel sorry for myself. So, with a sheepish, head hanging, eyes on the floor look, I approached my mother about my problem (I would never have told my dad about this; this was way too embarrassing). With hesitation, I slowly removed my sock to reveal my bright red toenails to my mom. Oh brother, she laughed and laughed! I made her promise to never EVER tell my father. I'm sure she kept that secret! Anyway, the secret's out and hopefully he never reads this book, though that is not likely either.

I tell you this story not only to publically repent of such a heinous act, but to remind you that my convictions of what biblical manhood is have come not by study alone but through experience. So let me begin by asking the question, "What is manhood?

The Abolition of Manhood

Contrary to popular belief, being a man is hard work. Yet today, the common view of men is that we are lazy, naïve, and hormonally-challenged. Television shows and movies portray us as sweat-pants-wearing, sex-craved, TV-lounging, beer-consuming, sports fanatics who treat women like dogs and dogs like kings. Also, radio talk shows portray us as Neanderthals who know nothing about women except the number of them with whom we have slept. Have you ever heard of Howard Stern? Stern is one of the most recognized voices on the radio, and he prides himself on sexual content.

Is this what being a man is all about?

Browsing a display of popular magazines ignites and fuels the very thoughts Christian men ought to control. The covers of magazines show us exactly what popular culture believes concerning sex. They are all about positions, sex tips, getting a six-pack, pseudo-romantic love interests, and Hollywood sex gossip. Spending the day on a major university campus gives us an even larger glimpse of how young people view manhood and womanhood. Within fraternity walls and college dorm rooms, men treat women as objects. This happens not only within fraternity and sorority walls but also in homes, schools, bars, dance clubs, work places, and, sadly, even in Bible-believing churches.

Men neglect their true responsibilities as men.

WE HAVE BEEN SO influenced by our culture that even marriage is now seen through the lens of the culture instead of through the lens of Scripture. Young people are very sexually active and are pushing marriage off until later in life. According to the Kaiser Family Foundation:[2]

- The median age at first intercourse is 16.9 years for boys and 17.4 years for girls.
- Over half of males (55%) and females (54%) ages 15 to 19 report having had oral sex with someone of the opposite sex. Approximately one in ten males and females ages 15 to 19 have engaged in anal sex with someone of the opposite sex. Three percent of males ages 15 to 19 have had anal sex with a male.
- The percentage of high school students who report having had four or more sexual partners declined in recent years from 18% in 1995 to 14% in 2005. Males (17%) are more likely than females (12%) to report having had four or more sexual partners.
- Among those ages 20 to 24, males have a higher average number of partners (3.8) than females (2.8). Men in this age group are also more likely (30%) than women (21%) to report having had seven or more sexual partners.
- Approximately nine out of ten men (89%) and women (92%) ages 22 to 24 have had sexual intercourse.

---

[2] Kaiser Family Foundation Statistics, http://www.kff.org/womenshealth /upload/3040-03.pdf.

- The average age of first marriage has risen by over a year for both men and women since 1990, reaching 26 for women and 27 for men in 2003, suggesting that many young people have sex before they are married.

According to the US Census Bureau's website, as of 2012, the average age of first marriage in 2010 was 28 for men and 26 for women. Although the trends seem to not be so drastic over the past 100 or so years (25 being the average age for men and 21 the average for women), this does suggest that young people have been delaying marriage for some time now and could possibly be one of the reasons that over 90% of twenty-somethings have had sexual intercourse outside of marriage today.

What's more, the evidence is everywhere. Turn on the television. Watch a movie. Open up the computer screen. Walk on a college or university campus. For instance, have you ever seen the television show *Two and a Half Men*? The whole show is about two idiots who teach a soon-to-be idiot about what being a "man" is. Ashton Kutcher's character, formally Charlie Sheen's character, teaches his nephew Jake about sex and relationships by bringing home young girls every weekend that can't complete a full sentence, and they often use big words such as 'like' and 'totally' every other word. Jake's dad is no different. Both so-called men are sleazeballs and both are loved by the men in our culture. Our culture's portrayal of manhood, through popular media like TV, movies, and the radio, stands in stark contrast with manhood according to God's word.

Also, some common cultural presuppositions for stereo-typing married men are that we either work hard for success and financial freedom, often at the cost of neglecting our families, or we are lazy and sit around all day while we should be out working hard to provide financially for our families. I am currently thinking of the examples of Michael Jordan and Homer Simpson.

MJ was my hero when I was a kid. Seriously, I loved him! I collected all the cards, slept in his jersey, and never missed a game! When I was only 9, he came out of his first retirement and started wearing #45 instead of #23. The day the #45 jersey went on sale, I took all my money that I had saved up, which was mostly pennies, nickels, dimes, and quarters, and I went to the mall and slammed that sack of coins on the counter with pride. Why? I wanted that #45 jersey! It's actually still hanging in my closet! He is, in my humble opinion, the greatest basketball player ever to lace 'em up. But being the best often comes with the neglect of something else. It's called opportunity cost. When you choose A you forfeit B. We'll talk more about that in Chapter 8. I am not discrediting MJ's undeniably amazing work ethic on and off the court, but the time and energy he placed toward hoops required the neglect of something great—his family. MJ and his wife divorced in 2006, which at the time became the most costly divorce in celebrity history with a settlement of $168 million for his wife.[3]

Homer Simpson, on the other hand, is the caricature of a lazy and stupid man who can't control his temper, wears dirty sweat pants all day, and often bursts out in anger. He is negligent, selfish, and out of shape. He sits around all day, sleeps when he should be working, complains even when there is nothing to complain about, and always gets into mischief.

What I am not saying is that all men are like this, though I am saying that this is our culture's commonest portrayal of us. We are either over-achievers who never see our families or lazy bums whom our families wish weren't around so often! So, why has the priority of biblical manhood disintegrated over the recent years? And, why has the view of manhood, as it is currently defined and portrayed by our culture, evolved the way it has?

Men Without Chests

IT IS TRUE and the saying is trustworthy—men transmit manhood to other men. What does this say about former and current generations? Where have we gone wrong? The intellectual giant, C.S. Lewis, says in *The Abolition of Man* that we have created men without chests. Lewis argues that the educational system of his day was *making* men without chests by teaching them inappropriate emotional responses. Teachers transmit

[3]Fox News Story - http://www.foxnews.com/story/0,2933,266343,00.html

not only instruction but also action and emotion. According to Lewis, for the Christian,

> You must train in the pupil those responses which are in themselves appropriate, whether anyone is making them or not, and in making which the very nature of man consists.[4]

For the non-Christian, or the one who does not hold to objectivity or meaning, which Lewis refers to as the *Tao*, he says,

> If they are logical, they must regard all sentiments as equally non-rational, as mere mists between us and the real objects. As a result, they must either decide to remove all sentiments, as far as possible, from the pupil's mind; or else to encourage some sentiments for reasons that have nothing to do with their intrinsic 'justness.' The latter course involves them in the questionable process of creating in others by 'suggestion' or incantation a mirage which their own reason has successfully dissipated.[5]

According to Lewis, the educational system was progressing into the latter and in so doing was making men without chests. Lewis gives us a grand analogy that might help us better understand what he is saying.

> When a Roman father told his son that it was a sweet and seemly thing to die for his country, he be-

---

[4]CS Lewis, *The Abolition of Man*, 20-21.

[5]Ibid.

> lieved what he said. He was communicating to the son an emotion which he himself shared and which he believed to be in accord with the value which his judgment discerned in noble death.[6]

When men train younger men to have appropriate emotional responses, such as a nobility and honor in dying for one's country, the very nature of what a man is becomes evident. When men transmit what a man is supposed to be to other men, manhood then becomes objective and appropriate emotional responses to things also become objective for all men. This is only the case if absolute truth exists. As Christians, if we believe that the Bible is truth, then we believe it gives us instructions for all of life. This includes marriage, biblical womanhood, and biblical manhood, or as some might say—gender roles. When we cultivate a biblical worldview we then better understand God's ultimate design for both men and women in singlehood, marriage, the family, and the church. Godly men must teach boys how to be godly men. The quote at the beginning of this chapter is ever pertinent now:

> In a sort of ghastly simplicity we remove the organ and demand the function. We make men without chests and expect of them virtue and enterprise. We laugh at honour and are shocked to find traitors in our midst. We castrate and bid the geldings be fruitful.[7]

---

[6]Ibid.

[7]Ibid., 26.

Somewhere along the line, older men have stopped teaching younger men what true biblical manhood is. Manhood has been abolished. Culture is now king. Popular culture defines what a man is supposed to be. We give into the lusts of our flesh and we justify it by seeing men all over the place who act just like us. We have no chests. No heart. No courage. We don't understand what it means to be a leader, provider, and protector. We don't develop appropriate emotional responses to being a leader, provider, and protector. It takes us three months to make an easy decision. We don't work hard, and we spend the majority of our time doing brainless activities that make our bellies bigger and our pants tighter. This must change! Yes, we are products of our cultural frameworks, but that does not mean our worldview has to be. Let us not be men without chests! We must go forth intentionally! We must be men with iron chests!

Men with Iron Chests

As stated above, we can only practice this approach to manhood if truth exists. As Christians, we believe that God is the Creator of all truth and that he has revealed this truth in his Word, and ultimately, in the person and work of Jesus.[8] God has revealed himself to his people in Scripture. Through Scripture, Christians

[8]Hebrews 1:1-3.

are given instructions and guidelines on how to relate not only to their Creator but also to each other. The Bible teaches us how to relate to each other as men and women using proper gender roles—the roles and characteristics that men and women are supposed to embody according to Scripture. When gender roles are practiced properly, men and women complement each other in accordance with God's will. This is the theological position known as complementarianism. Men and women *complement* each other according to their designed purpose.

Very early in Scripture we learn that both men and women are created in the image of God. Genesis 1:27 says, "So God created man in his own image, in the image of God he created him; male and female he created them." Everything that encompasses both men and women reflects the very nature of God. I am not saying that God, the Father, is both masculine and feminine, because he is not. God is very masculine. God is always referred to as Father in Scripture—never mother. I am saying we are made to be like him. We are relational; we have cognitive abilities; we can be creative, etc. We reflect God in these ways. He lives in community with himself in the triune Godhead as Father, Son, and Holy Spirit. The Trinity is one God manifested in three persons. One of the most amazing things about the Trinity is the fact that each person in the Godhead relates to each other in complete complementary ways. The Father is the head and supreme authority; the Son submits to the Father's ultimate will and works to glorify the Father even as he is exalted at the Father's right hand; and the Holy Spirit works in congruence with both the Son and the Father to accomplish the Father's designed purpose for his creation.

Before sin was in the world, Adam and Eve related to each other perfectly. Their intrinsic value as a man and woman were summed up in the fact that they were made in God's image and after his own likeness, and that everything in the world was good, as there was yet no sin. When sin entered into the world everything was shattered. Not only were men separated from God but also their relationships with one another were no longer perfect.

Very early in the story of human history it seems that all was lost. We are left with a man and a woman in broken relationship with one another, both of which have been separated from their Creator. One of my favorite things about Scripture is that sorrow, brokenness, and sin often set the stage for glorious redemption. In Genesis 3:15 we read that God will not abandon his people. This is often said to be the first gospel promise. God makes a promise with the serpent that he will one day crush his head through the woman's offspring. Throughout the Old Testament, God is faithful to this promise and sets the stage for this glorious redemption. The man who crushes the head of the serpent is a great King. His name is Jesus. He is the perfect man. Jesus defeated sin at the cross, and he defeated death when he rose from the dead. In Acts 1, we read of Jesus ascending to the Father's right hand to be exalted.

The Apostle Paul says this in 1 Corinthians 11:3: "But I want you to understand that the head of every man is Christ, the head of a wife is her husband, and the head of Christ is God." In this verse, Paul clearly defines the structure of relationships not only as they relate to the Trinity but also regarding the husband and wife in marriage. The important thing to notice is the fact that the relationship between husband and wife should reflect the relationship between Christ and the Church *and* the relationship between God the Father and Jesus, God the Son. The head of every man is Jesus. As stated above, he is the perfect man, and the head of all humanity. Christ is also the head of his body, the church. We will come back to this in greater detail later.

In marriage, the husband is the head of the home. Played out in everyday life this means that the husband is the primary authority in the home, though this does not mean that he is a dictator. Those guys who think that they are king of their castle should be taken to the proverbial woodshed and be taught a lesson or two. We will also come back to this in detail.

Being the head of your home means that you are a humble leader and servant, a hard worker, and a courageous protector. It does not mean that you boss around your family and expect them to rub your feet at the snap of the finger. Men and women are equal in dignity, value, and worth, but they are different in function.

Complementarians also believe that gender roles exist not only in the family and in life itself, but also in the life of the church. Logically, if the church is made up of families and the man is the head of the family then it only seems plausible that a man would lead in the church as well. We will come back to this in Chapter 4. As for now, the point is clear: *God has designed gender roles for both men and women, and we are created in his image.*

When Christian men transmit what biblical manhood is to young men, these young men then begin to develop in themselves what a true man is supposed to be, one with appropriate emotional responses according to Scripture. We no longer have inappropriate responses to members of the opposite sex, to football games,[9] to success and money, or to our families. Again, the saying is true and trustworthy: older men must teach and train younger men how to be men.[10]

If older men do not teach and train younger men what biblical manhood is, then we have simply removed the heart and demanded the functions—courage, leadership, provision, protection, decision-making, etc.[11] Men, and Christian men at that, devel-

---

[9]Let me be clear, I love football and all that is sport! I am not a fanatic, but I am a fan! My point is concerning an inappropriate emotional response to football when it is elevated to idolatry and above our duties as men.

[10]Titus 2:1-10

[11]It seems now that we no longer demand the functions of manhood either.

op wrong emotional responses to life and the duties before them as men created in the image of God.[12] Christian men must step up and be men, not according to what the culture says a man is, but according to what the Bible alone says a man must be. Another way of stating this is to urge men to develop a mature sense of masculinity.

In his book with Wayne Grudem, *Recovering Biblical Manhood and Womanhood*, John Piper gives this definition of 'mature masculinity.' He says, "At the heart of mature masculinity is a sense of benevolent responsibility to lead, provide for, and protect women in ways appropriate to a man's differing relationships."[13] The word benevolent simply means kindly or charitably and without any form of personal profit. Men must intrinsically act this way toward women. Again, we will also discuss this in much more detail in the chapters to come.

But for now let me give you my working definition of biblical manhood:

> A biblical man, marked with courage, is a leader, provider, and protector. He pursues his family, serves his church, shares and defends truth, makes good decisions, and redeems his time. And then teaches other men to do the same.

The purpose of this book is to champion this type

---

[12]Genesis 1:26

[13]John Piper and Wayne Grudem. *Recovering Biblical Manhood & Womanhood: A Response to Evangelical Feminism,* 35-45.

of preparation and courageous approach while also providing some biblically based applications for which to strive towards. We must become men who run after the benevolent responsibility of caring for women, children, and the needy. Let me be clear, if you are a man who is reading this book, I challenge and urge you to pursue this courageous approach to biblical manhood that I have laid out in the following pages. Throw away the cultural skirt and stop walking around like a man without a chest. Pursue biblical manhood. Pursue truth. Pursue Jesus. Become a man with an iron chest who can make a decision, protect women and children, strive for holiness, redeem his time, and lead and serve like Jesus.

So, why was I so embarrassed about painting my toenails red? Why did I hide it from my dad? Why didn't I just flaunt my pretty little red toes like it was normal for a boy to wear that stuff?

The answer: men don't paint their toenails.

There is a specific way designed by God for a man to act like a man, and vice versa for women. Toenail polish, dresses, and tight pants are not necessarily feminine in and of themselves. The object is neither feminine nor masculine. It is an object; it is a thing. Though the action behind these objects and the way we use them are strictly feminine in our culture. In our culture dresses are feminine objects. Toe nail polish is a feminine object.

Men, we must distinguish ourselves from that

which is feminine in our culture. We must not blur the lines.

As Christian men and women, we must teach our children at an early age what biblical femininity and masculinity are. We must teach our little girls about the essence of what makes a girl beautiful. We must teach our little boys about the roles of men and what makes a man masculine. Sports are not necessarily a 'boy' thing either.

Girls can play sports and still have a feminine persona about them. Girls can be helicopter pilots and still be feminine. Guys can cut hair and still be masculine. But girls should not try to act like men, and guys should not act like women.

As men and women, we are made in the image God—both male and female. We have been given gender roles to reflect the communal aspect of the Trinity. When men act like men and women act like women they then most reflect God's intended design for his most prized possessions.

When boys, or men, paint their toenails they reflect femininity, which by logical comparison is not what a young man should be learning about God's design for him.

Thankfully, my parents never painted my toenails. Only I was that stupid!

It is curious that physical courage should be so common in the world and moral courage so rare.
MARK TWAIN

—CHAPTER TWO—

BOOT CAMP

Learning to Develop Courage for All of Life's Tasks

LIKE MOST YOUNG men today, when I was a child and even a teenager, my primary view of courage was Mel Gibson walking around with war paint on his face and a sword in his hand as he bravely and heroically went into battle in the movies *Braveheart* and *The Patriot.*

I will not hesitate to say that this is still the common view concerning the virtue of courage in our culture today.

According to our culture, courage is primarily viewed as the action of carrying your sword into a fight with a little bit of blood dripping from your cheek. In other words, when we think of courage it is often through the lens of movies like the ones mentioned above. I'm currently thinking of the movie *300*. In this movie, you've got warriors that are portrayed as deadly, killing machines.

It is often the case that courageous endeavors sing to hearts of men quicker and stronger than any other action. Displays of strength, honor, and courage leave men gasping for more, and more often than not, leave lasting awe-inspiring and jaw-dropping impressions in our minds—and honestly, on our hearts. We love awesome displays of physical courage. We love guys who can hold their own, whether it's on the battlefield, the basketball court, or in the UFC octagon.

In 2009, I attended my brother-in-law's Marine Corps Officer Candidate School (OCS) graduation in Quantico, Virginia. If you have ever been to one of these ceremonies then you know what I mean when I say that these graduations just fire you up. But first, let me tell you a little bit about the men on my wife's side of the family for clarification. My oldest brother-in-law, Luke, is an officer in the Navy, and Isaac, the second oldest brother, is an officer in the Marine Corps. I love these men (three brothers in all), and they are definitely heroes of mine for what they do every day.

When this side of the family gets together for holidays, we don't just sit around and relax, watch movies, or fiddle our thumbs. Oh no! We drink protein shakes, participate together in extreme bodyweight workouts where we do massive amounts of pushups, pull-ups, and dips, and have high intensity pull-up competitions!

Yes, when the Riddle men get together it is then time to individually display our feats of strength to one another. We are men. It would be weird if we didn't do that. I'm not singling out just my family either, but this is how men are. We love competition that allows us to display our strength and physical attributes to other people. We are wired that way.

There is something fascinating to me about being on a military base. Maybe it's the intentional displays of propaganda or maybe it's just seeing men become soldiers and train to be warriors, but needless-to-say, it sings to my heart. What struck me the most were the discipline that these men carried themselves with, as well as the way they presented themselves. The man who spoke, a general of sorts, was a man who demanded your respect from the time he walked into the room until the time he left. Not because he asked for it, no, but because everybody in the room, including the civilians, *wanted* to give it to him. You could see by the way he presented himself that he was a man worthy of respect. The other men sat at ease, though to me it looked like "at attention," holding their backs completely straight and attentively giving him locked-in eye contact. The general spoke to the soon-to-be officers about honor, courage, integrity, and what it means to be a warrior *and* a gentleman. I left the OCS graduation that day with the utmost desire to be an officer in the military. Man, I was pumped up and ready to join right then! Why? Because everything they seemed to do, all the ways in which they presented themselves, and everything this general talked about reflected my desires, values, and intrinsic wiring as a man. I mean, my two favorite movies are *Gladiator* and *Braveheart.* Honor, integrity, and courage are virtues that sing to my heart, and the best thing about the general's speech was that he paralleled courage *in action* with the courageous approach to *walking in integrity.*

Not every day do we get to see the virtue of courage displayed in love, speech, and morality, because as stated above, our culture primarily portrays courage as a robust physical act. But contrary to culture, the Bible shows us that manhood is not just found in physical acts of courage, but also in speech and morality as well. When we do this, we then reflect a courageous God that fights for his people, sacrificially loves us, presents and reveals his character through the written Word, and displays his actions and character as both completely loving and completely just.

Courage Displayed in Action

THE BOOK OF JOSHUA presents a man who believed the LORD when the LORD said to him that he would give him every place that his foot landed upon.[1] The LORD continued to promise him that no man would be able to stand against him, and that the

[1]Joshua 1:3.

LORD would be with him all of his days.[2] This book's namesake, Joshua, was in fact that man. He was the son of Nun, who was Moses' servant.[3] Joshua stepped into the shoes of the greatest leader in all of Israel's history up to that point, and God called him out to take Israel into the Promised Land. For Joshua, there were only 2 requirements: 1) He must be strong and courageous,[4] and 2) he must meditate on the Torah day and night and be careful to do what it required.[5]

The story goes on to tell of a courageous man who loved God and bravely led his warriors into battle after battle in the hopes that they would soon be able to possess and inhabit the Promised Land, just as God had promised their father Abraham.[6] And in faithfulness to his covenant promise with Abraham, God fulfilled his covenant (though now that we have full revelation we know that the Promised Land is ultimately fulfilled in the New Heavens and New Earth at the time of Jesus' return). Joshua, as God promised him, led Israel into the Promised Land of Canaan, a land flowing with milk and honey.

It is interesting to note that four times in the first eighteen verses of the book of Joshua, God urged Joshua to be strong and courageous. God could have told Joshua anything in the world when he stepped into the shoes of Moses to lead the people of Israel, but he told

---

[2]Joshua 1:5.
[3]Joshua 1:1.
[4]Joshua 1:6, 7, 9, and 18.
[5]Joshua 1:8.
[6]Genesis 12-17.

him four times to have courage and to be strong. The story of Joshua's leadership over Israel is one of my favorite narratives in all of Scripture. It constantly reminds me of the tremendous courage that Joshua portrayed when time after time he risked his life to lead his people into battle. I may not be leading people into war, but as a Christian man there are many times when I need to possess the virtue of courage, whether it's boldly proclaiming the gospel, standing up in front of a crowd to preach, defending the truth of the gospel to skeptics and unbelievers, or protecting my family during times of trouble, other women according to my relationship with them, and the needy by putting myself in between them and harm.

Let me be clear, you *must* possess courage to be a leader.

Courage is often defined as the action of doing something that is against the status quo. According to Webster, courage is defined as "mean, mental, or moral strength to resist opposition, danger, or hardship. Courage implies firmness of mind and will in the face of danger or extreme difficulty <the *courage* to support unpopular causes>."[7] This action could be defined as anything risking your own life for the sake of something or someone else to firmly standing up for a conviction. And more often than not, when you pursue a courageous action it comes with those uneasy nerves or that bad feeling you get in your stomach when your

---

[7]The Merriam-Webster English Dictionary: New Edition, 2004.

little brother is about to tattle on you for calling him a bad name.

Overcoming Fear & Nervousness

SOME PEOPLE CALL these bad feelings butterflies and some refer to them as just being afraid—both are probably right. But let me ask you a question: Just because something makes you nervous, does that mean you shouldn't partake in it? Absolutely not! Many times as men we fail at courageous actions just because we are scared. We must overcome this pansy-like behavior.

As men, we must overcome our nervousness and anxiety.

Some of you might disagree with this, but we must teach young guys to engage in actions that might make them a little scared. In doing so, we teach them that just because they might feel scared does not mean they should not pursue the action.[8] Many young boys don't have a problem with this as it seems natural for them to explore and seek out adventure, but we must cultivate in them and in ourselves the ability to overcome fear.

For instance, think about the concept of shooting guns. If you have never been around guns, they probably make you a little nervous. But does this mean that you should not be around them or shoot them for rec-

---

[8] I learned this concept from sitting in a seminary class with Dr. Randy Stinson of the Southern Baptist Theological Seminary.

reation? I promise you, a good way to overcome fear and trepidation is to go do just that—shoot a gun… preferably a shotgun. When you first shoot a gun, your hands will probably be sweating, your heart will be pounding, and you will more than likely have that bad feeling in your stomach, but that doesn't mean it is a bad thing. Or, what about riding a motorcycle or a bike with no training wheels or rock climbing or backpacking or skiing or snowboarding? All of these activities would make the first time participant pretty nervous, but being nervous is no excuse for not participating.

We must cultivate this kind of behavior in young men—in all men. But let me be clear, we must always use wisdom in our courageous endeavors, and just because it seems like a good idea does not always make it the wisest decision. For instance, one time I was backpacking in the Smoky Mountains and I came upon a pretty steep rock wall. Obviously, the first thing that went through my mind when I saw this thing was, "I've got to climb it!"

Okay, this is what I mean by a courageous endeavor not being a good idea.

Without hesitation *or brains*, I took my pack off and began to climb. I got about 25 feet up the rock and realized that I couldn't get back down. Remember, I just happened to come across this rock wall and I didn't have any gear with me. As I free climbed this wall, and the higher and higher I ascended, it became foolishly apparent to me that I didn't have a harness, any rope, or even a helmet on. If I had fallen then I might have gone to see Jesus. I ended up getting down, but not without a few bumps and bruises and a little bit of blood.

I would recommend all young guys who are reading this book to find an older guy to participate in these kinds of activities with. Allow him to teach you the ropes first before you dive in and have no idea what you are doing. Doing that often causes disaster, and part of being a man is making wise and quick decisions and learning from your stupid mistakes, as well as those of others.

Overcoming nerves by participating in the activities mentioned above is a good way to prepare you to have courage when it really matters. What if you were drafted into the military to participate in war one day? What if someone or something was putting your family in danger? What if someone came into your home in the middle of the night? What if you had to get up in front of a crowd of people to speak? What happens when the time comes to pursue a beautiful lady for marriage? Will you just send her a text or shoot her an email like a little sissy? What happens when you have to go to your first job interview? OR, better yet, what happens when you have to face the scary task of asking your girlfriend's dad if you can marry his daughter? Even better, what if you had the perfect opportunity to share Jesus with somebody? Would you have the courage to do these things? These are serious situations that we must face in life, if you haven't already.

Remember, just because you are scared or nervous does not mean it is wrong!

A Steady Hand & Voice Goes Along Way

WHEN WE FIRST start participating in things that make us a little scared or nervous, most of the time, others can see it all over us. We begin to stutter; our voices begin to crack; our hands shake a little bit; our eye contact might be non-existent; and we are as tense as Bill Clinton when Monica Lewinsky walks into the room. As men, when we find ourselves in uncomfortable situations (and this will happen often) we must begin to practice presenting ourselves in honorable ways. First of all, we must begin to practice good eye contact. Honestly, I struggle with this, but I intentionally work on it every day. In the past, when I would talk to someone I would look at everybody or everything but the person I was talking with. Especially when I was nervous, I would look all over the room and never glance at the person I was speaking to. I've gotten better at this but it is still a struggle. Secondly, relax yourself. When you relax yourself you then begin to notice that everything else becomes much easier. Your hands will stop shaking and your voice will become steady. When others see a cool, calm, and collected man amidst something that would make them noticeably nervous it then helps them calm themselves and not become anxious either. And even if your heart continues to pound and you get a little scared, it's okay… just become really good at hiding it.

A good rule of thumb to live by is this: if you are in a leadership position and don't know what you are doing, always act like you know what you are doing, and most of the time, people will never even know it.

Having Courage Amidst Confrontation

FOR MOST PEOPLE there is never a time when courage is needed more than when confrontation looms. Men, I must tell you, confrontation *will* happen. What will separate you as a man who practices biblical manhood is how you handle confrontation when it takes place.

One thing is for certain, you must not run from it.

Part of being a man is dealing with confrontation, and at times, dealing with other people's confrontations that most of the time does not even involve you.

Whether it's with your family, church members, friends, or coworkers, confrontation will soon happen. One thing I would recommend when dealing with confrontation is to never handle it in rash moments. When this occurs, you are more than likely to say something you will regret. Remove yourself from the situation, think about what just occurred, and then proceed if need be. Also, it might be wise to get counsel during big confrontations.[9]

---

[9]The best resource I know about for studying and thinking through how to deal with conflict is the book *Crucial Confrontations: Tools for Talking About Broken Promises, Violated Expectations, and Bad Behavior* by Kerry Patterson, Joseph Grenny, Ron McMillan, and Al Switzler.

Remember, there was never anyone more confrontational then Jesus Christ himself. During his ministry we read of him confronting person after person with their sinful words and/or actions. In fact, the phrase, "Repent and believe, for the Kingdom of God is at hand," is one of the most controversial things you could say to someone today in our postmodern culture. Though this may be the case, we are called to have courage and boldly proclaim the gospel of Jesus Christ to all people. Can this be said about you?

Courage Displayed in Speech

WINSTON CHURCHILL once said, "Courage is what it takes to stand up and speak; courage is also what it takes to sit down and listen."[10] What a statement! We must learn when to stand up and speak and when to sit down and listen. It might not always be appropriate for us to speak, however, we must have courage to do either task. As stated above, a Christian man must have courage to boldly proclaim the gospel; it takes some boldness to share something that can be so offensive. In Acts 17, Paul gives us a great example of what having courage means when you are engaging people with the gospel. While Paul was in Athens he began to notice that the city was just absolutely full of idols. The Bible says that Paul's spirit was provoked within him because of this, and he then began to reason in the

---

[10]Attributed to Winston Churchill at a conference in Washington, DC.

synagogues with the Jewish leaders and devout religious people there. Not only did he reason in the synagogues, but he also began to reason in the marketplaces. Everywhere Paul went he began to *reason*. The word *reason* simply means to engage people with the gospel. Whether it is intellectual or not, when you reason with somebody you are simply engaging their heart and mind with the gospel of Jesus. It is almost like an argument.

It wasn't all fun and games for Paul. As he began to reason with the people in Athens, some of the more prominent philosophers of the day began to call him out, even calling him a "blabber" of sorts. They thought he was crazy. Why? Because he was preaching Jesus and the resurrection! You will always come across people who think you are crazy for believing in Jesus and wanting to share his message with them. Let me give you an example.

When I was living in Louisville, KY, I worked at a country club down on the Ohio River as a server. If you have never worked in a restaurant before then you are not really missing out on anything. Restaurants house some of the craziest people you will ever meet. It's a proven fact. They are crazy! One day, I struck up a conversation with one of our cooks in the kitchen about the gospel. We began to talk about the existence of God. During this particular conversation he asked me how in the world I could ever believe in such a crazy story. I asked him what he meant. He said, "Let me get this straight. You are telling me that God created the world good but man fell into 'sin,' and then Jesus, God's Son, came to die for us? That is just crazy. I can't believe you think that is actually true!" We began to discuss how he thinks there is no such thing as sin and how Christianity is this age-old religion that is based upon an ancient Babylonian myth. We agreed to exchange some material with each other. I agreed to watch this absolutely stupid YouTube video if he would read the Gospel of John. We agreed to get back together and talk about what we had watched and read. As I began to leave the kitchen he said something to me that I will never forget. He said, "Greg, I just want you to know that I am really good at talking people out of being a Christian." Obviously, he wasn't that good at it.

After these prominent philosophers began to notice Paul's *crazy* message they then brought him before the Areopagus. The court of the Areopagus of Athens was kind of like the House of Representatives and the Senate today if there was no separation of church and state. It had authority over all the civil and religious life of the day. When Paul spoke to them he was bold, but he was also loving. He spoke truth boldly to the main civil and religious leaders of his time. *Take time to read Acts 17 and study how Paul boldly proclaimed the gospel to the prominent philosophers of his day.*

Also, in Ephesians 4:22-32, Paul exhorts the church in Ephesus on how to live a godly life that parallels Christ's life. He says,

> Therefore, having put away falsehood, let each one

> of *you speak the truth with his neighbor*, for we are members one of another. Be angry and do not sin; do not let the sun go down on your anger, and give no opportunity to the devil. Let the thief no longer steal, but rather let him labor, doing honest work with his own hands, so that he may have something to share with anyone in need. *Let no corrupting talk come out of your mouths, but only such as is good for building up, as fits the occasion, that it may give grace to those who hear.* And do not grieve the Holy Spirit of God, by whom you were sealed for the day of redemption. Let all bitterness and wrath and anger and clamor and slander be put away from you, along with all malice. Be kind to one another, tenderhearted, forgiving one another, as God in Christ forgave you (emphasis mine).

In this passage we seem to be presented with both having the courage and boldness to present Christ to our neighbor, as well as having the courage and boldness to be holy in our speech. One thing I have noticed about men is that we are eager to engage in impure conversation. Even as Christians, we often joke around using sexual references and course joking. This is often the case with younger guys as pop culture flaunts this kind of conversation and it is marketed directly to our younger generation.

The book of Proverbs speaks numerous times concerning the use of wisdom with our *words* and using discernment about the *words* of others: a lying tongue is wicked (6:17); beware of the smooth tongue of an adulterous woman (6:24); the tongue of the righteous is choice silver (10:20); the perverse tongue will be cut off (10:31); rash words are like sword thrusts (12:18); the tongue of a wise man brings healing (12:18); truthful lips endure forever (12:19); the mouth of fools pour out folly (15:12); a gentle tongue is a tree of life (15:4); a dishonest tongue falls into calamity (17:20); death and life are in the power of the tongue (18:21); whoever keeps his mouth and his tongue keeps himself out of trouble (21:23); a lying tongue hates its victims (26:28). The book of James portrays the tongue as guiding the rest of the body as a small rudder guides a large ship.[11] James also refers to the tongue as a fire and a world of unrighteousness.[12]

It is crucial as we begin to practice biblical manhood that we have courage in our speech. Yes, we must have boldness in sharing God's Word, but we must also have holiness in our words towards others. There is a reason that James says the tongue is like a small fire that makes a large forest go up in flames. We must humble ourselves before God and be diligent in being cautious about the words we use towards others. Only through the power of the Holy Spirit in our lives will we be able to withstand causing these fires.

---

[11]James 1:4-5.
[12]James 1:6.

Courage Displayed in Morality

AN OFTEN FORGOTTEN form of courage is living in holiness. Men and women by nature are evil. David says in Psalm 51:5, "Behold I was brought forth in iniquity, and in sin did my mother conceive me." The reality is we don't need people to show us how to be evil because we are by nature evil. This is what is known as the doctrine of *total depravity*.[13] We don't need an Evil 101 class on how to lie, lust, covet, steal, cheat, and hate. Where there is no hint of gospel presence, men display iniquity without any form of direction. We do these things all the time... sometimes every day! In the gateway to the Psalter, Psalm 1:1-2, the psalmist gives us insight into walking in righteousness. He says, "Blessed is the man who walks not in the counsel of the wicked, nor stands in the way of sinners, nor sits in the seat of scoffers, but his *delight* is in the *law* of the LORD, and on his *law* he *meditates* day and night" (emphasis mine).

This is very similar language to that of Joshua 1, as I discussed above. Blessed is the man whose *delight* is in the law of God. According to the Psalmist, the righteous Israelite in the Old Testament would meditate on the Torah day and night. In this he would find joy. In this he would find delight, freedom, and liberty. In this he would experience God.

---

[13]The result of the fall of man in the Genesis 3 is what is known as total depravity. After sin entered into the world, all men, in Adam, are born as sinners. Contrary to some postmodern thought, humanity does not enter into this world inherently good. We are, by our sin nature, born as inherently evil and in need of a Savior.

This is a huge issue! Contrary to the popular ways in which men portray themselves in our culture today, a man who pursues this courageous approach to biblical manhood must courageously labor in living a moral life according to God's Word. It is only by meditating on Scripture and applying Scripture that we find the ability to live holy lives in the power of God, the Holy Spirit. As stated above, in this we find joy. In this we find delight. In this we experience God.

How can a young man keep his way pure? By guarding it according to the Word of God.[14]

Courage Often Leads to Influence

ONE NIGHT BACK when I was a youth intern at a church in Knoxville, TN, I found myself sitting at a minor league baseball game with about a hundred middle school students. I was sitting with one of my favorite students—Hackysack—and little did I know that night I would witness one of the greatest acts of influence I would ever see in a middle school kid. We called him Hackysack because all he wanted to do was play that silly game all the time. It was the bottom of the sixth inning, and as I sat in this hot, muggy stadium watching the game, Hackysack and one of his buddies got up and went to the restroom. Almost thirty minutes went by and Hackysack had yet to return from the restroom.

---

[14]Psalm 119:9.

At about the same time I began to worry about him, I began to hear a bunch of people screaming down at the bottom left of the stadium. We were all the way on the other side of the stadium in the general admission section.

After a closer look, I spotted my boy Hackysack, twelve years old, standing on a chair in front of thousands of people yelling: "ONE, TWO, THREEEE!" and then proceeded to watch thousands of people stand and do the wave. It was one of the greatest spectacles of courage I had ever witnessed in my life. Talk about *influence*! This twelve-year-old *influenced* a whole stadium to stand up and do the wave around the entire stadium multiple times.

All it took was a little bit of courage to get up in front of thousands of people and influence them to do what he wanted them to do. Imagine if we took that kind of courage and channeled it toward living courageously in action, speech, and morality for the glory of King Jesus.

I firmly believe that influence has a 360-degree tractor beam. When someone's thoughts and actions become reflective of Jesus then influence has a redemptive domino effect. It becomes attractive. Why? Because the courage it takes to live for Jesus in a postmodern world is completely opposite from what the world portrays as courage. It is courage displayed in action, speech, and morality. Opportunities present themselves every day for us to live courageously for Christ. Don't get me wrong, it will be hard, but it will be more rewarding than anything this world has to offer. So in the words of William Wallace, I ask you, "Are you ready for a war?"

Now if Christ is proclaimed as raised from the dead, how can some of you say that there is no resurrection of the dead? But if there is no resurrection of the dead, then not even Christ has been raised. And if Christ has not been raised, then our preaching is in vain and your faith is in vain.
PAUL, *1 Corinthians 15:12-14*

—CHAPTER THREE—

THE GOSPEL

Learning What I Must Believe, Know, & Defend

IN A CULTURE FULL of relativism and pluralism it is often thought to be lazy intellectualism to hold to any form of objective truth. Getting a college degree for young people today means coming to the conclusion that there may or may not be meaning at all. What is more, students are leaving colleges without holding to any form of absolute truth whatsoever, and ironically, they are *absolutely* sure about it!

Can this even be possible?

CS Lewis says this about a complete subjective and relative world,

> "You cannot go 'explaining away' forever; you will find that you have explained explanation itself away. You cannot go on 'seeing through' things forever.

The whole point of seeing through something is to see something through it. It is good that the window should be transparent, because the street or garden beyond it is opaque. How if you saw through the garden too? It is no use trying to 'see through' first principles. If you see through everything, then everything is transparent. But a wholly transparent world is an invisible world. To 'see through' all things is the same as not to see."[1]

If one looks up at the sky and refuses to acknowledge that the sky is actually there, it doesn't mean that the sky is not there. One is just refusing to acknowledge something that is objectively true. Similarly, many people refuse to believe in the God of the Bible, but just because they refuse to believe in him doesn't mean that he is not there and has not revealed himself in Scripture.

In today's culture, it is politically correct to think and live in pluralistic ways—as if there is no right and wrong. What is right for someone is right for him or her alone; what is right for another person is right for him or her alone as well. Who is to say what is right and what is wrong? Where is the foundation for morality? There is no "one way" to anything. People can take different routes to the same destination (i.e., multiple paths to God). There is no right way to raise your children. I actually had someone tell me one time that you

---

[1]CS Lewis. The Abolition of Man, 81.

shouldn't say "No" to your children because it seems to create a negative atmosphere and a negative persona about them.

Again, the ironic thing here is that this is simply lazy intellectualism and refusing to search out what is in fact objectively true. The question is not, "What (or who) is right and what (or who) is wrong," but rather, "What is truth?" When we come to a solid foundation for what truth is then we should begin to see all of life's questions and adventures through the lens of this truth.

This is where the gospel comes in. It is crucial that we as men understand the gospel and have the ability to defend it (1 Peter 3:15). The gospel gives the only sufficient answers to the hard questions of life, and it is the only thing that gives stability to guilt, meaning, and death. It is, in its simplest form, "good news." So, what is this good news?

At this point we must ask, "What is the gospel?" The gospel is the message of God, man, sin, Christ, and response. What is more, the gospel is the message that God, the Father, created the world good, and created humans in his image as very good. Man was created to be in relationship with his Creator and to give glory to him in all things, but early in the story man sinned by substituting himself for God and in so doing all of creation was affected. Sin in turn separated man from God. The rest of the story finds man in turmoil with God and in need of a Savior to pay the punishment for sin that man deserves. Man could not pay his own debt. Jesus, God the Son, then came to earth and lived a perfect life—because we could not—and died on a cross as a substitute for sin. In doing so, Jesus substituted himself for us, taking the punishment that we deserve—in the same way Adam substituted himself for God in the garden. Jesus arose from the dead, defeating death and ascended into Heaven at the Father's right hand. After taking his rightful place, Jesus sent God, the Holy Spirit, to call people to salvation, redeem cities and cultures, and build his church until he comes back. He is making all things new. Jesus, through the Spirit, is calling everybody everywhere to repent of all sin and to put their faith in him for the forgiveness of sin. Jesus will return, but he will not return empty handed. He will bring the New Heavens and New Earth. He will return as a Warrior King—one who completely defeats sin and death and ushers in the completeness of *shalom* (peace). He will then judge all people everywhere who have ever lived on earth, whether or not they have repented of sin and have put their faith in him. Jesus will then judge everybody who has ever lived. He will then graciously forgive those who do repent and punish those who do not by sending them to the real, eternal, and conscience torments of hell.

That is the gospel.[2]

It is also truth.

Just because someone refuses to believe the gospel

---

[2]A great book for understanding the gospel more is, *What is the Gospel?*, by Greg Gilbert.

does not mean that it is not true. Just like gravity; simply because someone refuses to believe in gravity does not make gravity not there. If one jumps, he will indeed fall.

Gravity is there and it is real.

One is simply refusing to see what is opaque and is looking at all things transparently, making the world invisible. However, what one refuses to see as opaque—the gospel—is the only thing that allows you to see everything else objectively. The gospel is the only lens that enables one to see the world as it is and as it should be (i.e., objectively).

I will argue that these truths above are the non-negiotables that one must believe in order to be a Christian, and really, these are the non-negotiables one must believe in order to be a man that practices biblical manhood.

It is interesting to me, that many men in the church cannot retain and restate this information. We have become so saturated with an easy believe-ism Christianity that is so popular these days. This has led men to their child-like understanding of what the gospel is, and has led many so-called men to compartmentalize everything they do. Men in our churches believe that Jesus is Lord, but they can't explain why. They go to church, but they can't tell you why! On Sundays, many of us go to church and participate in worship but on every other day of the week fail to demonstrate by our actions or speech that we are in fact followers of Jesus Christ. Is this true about us? Is this true about you? Do you love the gospel? Does your faith lack depth?

This is the underlying factor, and if we fall short of believing the gospel then we fall short of everything that is biblical manhood. This is number one. Here are a few things that we as biblical men *must* become.

1. We must be men who love the gospel.

ABOVE EVERYTHING ELSE, we must possess and hold tightly a dying love for the gospel of King Jesus! Men, it is not enough for us to be simply complacent in our churches and in our world today. The gospel is being attacked all over the place, and as stated above, especially on college and university campuses. Think about it this way: our young people are leaving our student ministries and churches without a firm understanding of Scripture. They can't defend why they believe what they believe, and in all honesty, it is still their parent's faith. When they go to college they are confronted with contrary beliefs and worldviews by professors who preach that truth is relative and there is no such thing as "one way" to God. Without a firm foundation and the ability to defend and understand what they believe, our young people begin to be swayed by the cultural, academic, and post-modern impetuses of our day.

A courageous approach to biblical manhood calls men to love the gospel with an uncanny passion. We must dive into God's Word daily, and we must always remind ourselves of God's grace in our lives. It is only through the gospel that we find a relationship with God, and it is only through a love for the gospel that we become men who begin to change the world and the status quos of our day!

2. We must be men who understand the gospel.

DON'T GET ME wrong; understanding the gospel and all of its implications is very hard work. Scripture is in fact an extremely hard book to fully comprehend. It's been 2,000 years and we are still trying to understand many theological issues in Scripture. It is no cakewalk, but it is *not* a daunting task either. There is a common characteristic amongst men in our culture today that we hate to read. Maybe we do, but that is no excuse for not being able to understand the Bible. You don't need a seminary education to understand and apply Scripture to your life. Being a man who loves God's Word is really the only prerequisite to being a man who begins to reform manhood in his life and in the lives of others. The rest of these qualities and skills can be learned, but loving Scripture is something that you must come to possess. We come to possess this quality by God's grace, yes, but also by having daily times in God's Word. When we are in Scripture more, we begin to desire more of it. Understanding Scripture, on the other hand, is learned. It comes one day at a time. The great thing about diving into Scripture daily is the delight of being able to understand God more and how he has revealed himself to us in Scripture. What an amazing truth that is.

The task of understanding the gospel is also the task of becoming a theologian. When we begin to understand God more through his Word we then begin to understand the task of progressive sanctification in our lives. We might not ever become theologians like John Piper, Al Mohler, or Wayne Grudem, but when we pursue the task of knowing God more through his revealed Word then we become theologians in our own right and at our own pace. I promise you, in today's culture you will be asked often about the reliability and historicity of the Bible. You will be asked multiple and endless apologetics questions concerning your faith. Will you be able to hold your own? Will you be able to answer them? Do you even know what *apologetics* means? Maybe you should start there.

3. We must be men who can teach the gospel to others.

THE APOSTLE PAUL says this in Titus 2:1-9, "But as for you, teach what accords with sound doctrine. Older men are to be sober-minded, dignified, self-controlled, sound in faith, in love, and in steadfastness… Likewise, urge the younger men to be self-controlled. Show yourself in all respects to be a model of good works, and in your *teaching* show integrity, dignity, and sound speech that cannot be condemned, so that an opponent may be put to shame, having nothing evil to say about us" (emphasis added). As we've discussed already, there is a crucial task that older men must pursue. They must teach younger men the ways of the faith. I cannot urge this enough. Young men must learn to walk in integrity, dignity, and have sound speech from older men. We learn manhood and *truth* from those who teach it to us. Older men must model this in their lifestyle and in their *teaching*.

What do we teach? It is simple—we teach the gospel! We must teach the gospel when we drive down the road, when we sit with our families at the dinner table, when we are spending time with our children, and obviously, when we teach and preach. I know that most men will never stand up in front of crowds to preach the gospel, but we must be ready if the moment ever arises. The gospel is the central message in all of our teaching; it is the lens through which we view the rest of Scripture and the rest of the world.

4. We must be men who can defend the gospel.

ANOTHER WAY for men to possess courage is to stand up for what they believe in. We are at a crucial time in the history of America, as this once Christian land becomes a mission field again. In 1986, Lesslie Newbigin began to argue that Western society was in fact a mission field again.[3] Throughout church history, there have been times when the church was in serious decline. It was through revival though that society was reinvigorated with the gospel during these times. The difference between then and our present state is that culture today is no longer nominally Christian. Today there has been a comprehensive corrosion of truth and the reliability and authority of Scripture is no longer prominent.[4]

Things *are* different now. Tim Keller, in his contribution to, *The Supremacy of Christ in a Postmodern World*, says that this post-Christian society has developed 'antibodies' against full-blown Christianity.[5] It seems that truth is being attacked on every street corner, and often times it is through the subliminal messages that our media (TV, movies, radio, etc.) presents. Vodie Bauchum rightly states, "Truth is under attack in modern American culture. Rare is the person who believes that there are facts that correspond with reality (truths) and that those facts are true for all people in all places and at all times."[6]

All is not lost, though, as we venture into this postmodern movement. Collin Hansen's book, *Young, Restless, Reformed*, discusses the resurgence of Reformed

---

[3]Lesslie Newbigin, *Foolishness to the Greeks* (Grand Rapids, MI: Eerdmans, 1986) and *The Gospel in a Pluralistic Society* (Grand Rapids, MI: Eerdmans, 1989).

[4]John Piper, *The Supremacy of Christ in a Postmodern World*. Tim Keller, "The Gospel and the Supremacy of Christ" (Wheaton, IL: Crossway Books, 2007), 104.

[5]Ibid.

[6]Vodie Baucham, JR. *The Ever-Love Truth: Can Faith Thrive in Post-Christian Culture?* (Nashville, TN: Broadman & Holman Publishers, 2004).

theology among younger evangelical leaders. On the other hand, however, he discusses in an article he wrote on the same subject[7] the popularity of Emergent theology, which is perhaps most identified with Brian McLaren and Rob Bell.[8] I would caution all to be weary of their teachings, especially since McLaren's latest book denies everything that is essentially orthodox Christianity,[9] and Bell's latest book on Hell does the same.[10]

Men, we must see ourselves as missionaries to our culture. When we become complacent, we become the statistics I've spoken of throughout this book. Who's afraid of post-modernism? Men who love, understand, teach, and defend the gospel are armed and ready for battle. And we are not afraid!

God is too Big to Fit into One Religion

I WAS DRIVING down the road awhile ago with my wife and I noticed a bright red bumper sticker on the back of a hybrid, which said, "God is too big to fit into one religion!" We ended up pulling into the same parking lot and parked close together. I really wanted to engage this person about their bold bumper sticker, and I wanted to probe their thoughts on such an interesting statement, however, she took off into one store as my wife and I ventured into another.

---

[7]Collin Hansen, "Young, Restless, Reformed," *Christianity Today* (September 2006).

[8]See http://emergentvillage.com.

[9]Brian McLaren, *A New Kind of Christianity: Ten Questions that are Transforming the Faith* (New York, NY: HarperCollins Publishers, 2010).

[10]Rob Bell, *Love Wins* (New York, NY: HarperCollins, 2011).

This did get me thinking though. What would she have said if I had inquired about her bumper sticker? Well, I'm pretty sure I know what she would have said, as the meaning of the bumper sticker is quite clear, but if truth is relative could the meaning of a bumper sticker also be relative?

Is there meaning in this bumper sticker?

The statement, "God is too big to fit into one religion," is probably the main presupposition of our generation. Why? Believing in something/anything is quite the fad these days. Atheism seems to be so last generation. Modernism is out the door and the search for "How do we know?" is in. It seems that everybody believes in "god," but when you throw in any form of exclusivity the door is shut and you are seen as judgmental and brainwashed. Believe me, I've been described as all these things and more. I was actually described the other day by a man twice my age as "a good kid," but he continued saying that I "just need a little direction in my life." Not because I was smoking weed or breaking down doors but because I believed in absolute truth… truth found in the Bible alone!

Unbelievable!

Here's the deal. The statement, "God is too big to fit into one religion," actually makes God rather small. When you make this claim you are making God into what you want him (or her or it) to be. God is not the big one. You are the big one. God has now become very small, smaller than each of us. God has now become small enough that we are able to fit him into our own desires and beliefs. In reality, if ten people make this claim then there are ten different gods out there, all smaller than the person who made this claim. Each god is different and each god is made in our image.

When we make this claim, we are making the god we want to exist, well… exist, so that we are able to justify how we want to live our lives. A murderer can form a god of murder and justify his actions. A rapist can form a god of rape and immediate satisfaction and fulfillment to justify his actions.

It's actually that simple.

Also, when we make this claim we often forget that every belief in a historical religion makes exclusive truth claims, and ironically, to make the statement, "God is too big to fit into one religion," is in fact an exclusive truth claim. It is self-defeating. Logically, this way of thinking leads to the statement that no God, or religion, should exist, because all religions should practice tolerance, but instead they all make exclusive claims about God and about truth.

Everybody wants to believe in "God," but nobody wants a God that demands anything from him. Nobody wants to be held accountable for his or her actions.

The God of the Bible is seen in Scripture as Creator, Ruler, Judge, and Savior. His name is Jesus.

He is the *Creator* of the entire world. He *Rules* over all of creation, all peoples, all cultures, and all religions. He will one day *judge* everybody who has ever lived,

NOT on whether they have been good or bad (he is not Santa Clause), but whether they have repented of sin and have believed in him as Savior and King. What is more, he is the *Savior* of the world—he is a God who saves. Jesus is a big God. He is not a little god that lives on a bumper sticker or a little god that is created in our image to justify our actions and the way we want to live. He is worth following; he is worth defending. He is a God that demands obedience from his people—his church. He is God of gods and Lord of lords. He is not small.

Only small gods live on bumper stickers.

ONE DAY, THERE WILL no longer be a need for defending truth. This will be a glorious day. Trumpets will sound, mountains will shake, lions will lie down with lambs, and bodies will rise to meet their King! This day—the last day—Jesus will be completely exalted over all of creation. Sin will be no more; death will be no more. There will no longer be obnoxious bumper stickers (pluralistic or Christian). We will finally partake in the marriage supper of the Lamb, and we will gather together with all the saints and the four living creatures who gather around his throne and sing ever joyously, "Holy, holy, holy, is the LORD God Almighty, who was and is and is to come!" (Revelation 4:8).

What a glorious day that will be indeed! Though we

carry the burden of defense now, take hope! Look up! The Son of God will return! Let us be men who walk with this perspective.

"Now concerning the matters about which you wrote: 'It is good for a man not to have sexual relations with a woman.' But because of the temptation to sexual immorality, each man should have his own wife and each woman her own husband."
PAUL, *1 Corinthians 7:1-3*

—CHAPTER FOUR—

MARRIAGE

The Most Important Mission

IN A CULTURE WHERE sex is flaunted and success and money are the primary ends for which people live their lives, it is only reasonable that marriage would be placed on the back burner until later in life.

Opposing worldviews give us more than substantial reason and provide more than a solid foundation for why two people disagree. With multiple languages, ethnicities, cultures, philosophies, and religions alive in the world today, there are multiple frameworks, sometimes countless frameworks, in which people might approach truth issues. But for Christians, the Bible is the source of truth. The Bible's claim that its story is The Story is the foundational approach Christians should take in all the decisions they make. Even about marriage. Even about sex. Even about being a husband, father, and leader. Even about being a wife, mother, and nurturer.

At this time, let us revisit the statistics from the Kaiser Family Foundation that we read in chapter one,

- The median age at first intercourse is 16.9 years for boys and 17.4 years for girls.
- Over half of males (55%) and females (54%) ages 15 to 19 reports having had oral sex with someone of the opposite sex. Approximately 1 in 10 (11%) males and females ages 15 to 19 had engaged in anal sex with someone of the opposite sex; 3% of males ages 15 to 19 have had anal sex with a male.
- The percentage of high school students who report having had four or more sexual partners declined in recent years from 18% in 1995 to 14% in 2005. Males (17%) are more likely than females (12%) to report having had four or more sexual partners.
- Among those ages 20 to 24, males have a higher average number of partners (3.8) than females (2.8). Men in this age group are also more likely (30%) than women (21%) to report having had seven or more sexual partners.
- Approximately nine out of 10 men (89%) and women (92%) ages 22 to 24 have had sexual intercourse.

And the kickers…

- The average age of first marriage has risen by over a year for both men and women since 1990, reaching 26 for women and 27 for men in 2003, suggesting that many young people have sex before they are married.

According to the US Census Bureau, the average age of first marriage in 2010 was 28 for men and 26 for women.

In interpreting the statistics above, I am a strong advocate for young men and women dating intentionally for short periods of time and getting married early rather than later in life.

In a discussion worth quoting in full on a "single's sense of purpose,"[1] Vodie Baucham and Managing Editor of *Boundless* (a magazine for 20-somethings from Focus on the Family), Motte Brown, have some interesting things to say concerning early preparation for marriage. Brown says to Vodie, "You and your wife married as sophomores in college. And you mentioned elsewhere in your book that marriage is more important than college. Let's talk about when men should pursue marriage. I mean, would you recommend marriage to men who pursue dating relationships in college?" "First of all," says Vodie, "I would never recommend that anyone pursue a dating relationship. I believe dating is glorified divorce practice. You know,

[1] www.boundless.org

modern American dating has been disastrous. I believe in courtship: I believe courtship is for people who are ready to be married. And courtship is something that you enter into with the understanding that you're investigating toward marriage. Not just, you know, 'We're kicking it and then the next thing you know we spent all this time together; it seems like marriage ought to be the logical next step.' There are a lot of people who are in bad marriages because of that. It's kind of the default thing to do after they just hung out together for so long."

He continues: "The question of when to get married is not about age; it's about preparation. And the problem is that we're not doing any preparation. So when people hear about early marriage now in our culture, they think of the context of young men and women who haven't had any training or given any thought to marriage, and they go, "Wow! That's young." It is, well, if a person hasn't been given any training or any thought to marriage. So is 30, so is 40, if there hasn't been any training or any thought given to marriage. But if somebody understands what marriage is and they're being prepared for it, then really that's not young at all."

Motte then asks the million-dollar question. He says, "Of all the opportunities young adults have in front of them, what have you found to be the most rewarding priorities for them to set?"

"Marriage and family. Marriage and family," Vodie

says with much enthusiasm. "Because it is the most lasting, most life-impacting relationship that they will have outside of the one with their parents. It is. There is nothing that will be more lasting and more life impacting than that. That's why I make the statement about marriage being far more important than college. My marriage has shaped me as a man and as a follower of Christ far more than the time I spent in college did. And as far as the big picture, the long term, it will have much more impact than that."

I agree with Vodie completely.

Let's go back to C.S. Lewis' statement that he made forty years ago about the current educational system in London, when he said, "We are making men without chests." This statement applies today more than ever. In our homes and schools we are making men without chests (even if we unintentionally do so). We are not preparing young men to be husbands, leaders, providers, and protectors, but we are preparing them to be "successful" in the world's eyes.

We don't train them for marriage; we train them for college. Even in Christian homes, little if any preparation and training for marriage is attempted. Instead, young men and women are encouraged to pursue careers, money, and success, which are not necessarily bad things in and of themselves, but outside of an intentional preparation for marriage they lead to the statistics above… even for Christians.

Young men and women, it is only logical that you would begin to think about and prepare for marriage early! Older men, we must teach young people how to be leaders, providers, and protectors now. There is no time to wait! In a culture where there is so much immorality it is only inevitable that a young Christian man and a young Christian woman would engage in sexual acts. Think of it this way, a young man becomes sexually hormonal around the age of 13 or 14. If he gets married at the 'medium age above,' which is 27, then by simple math that is 13-14 years of living with intense sexual passions.

I know many men who have been intentional about marriage at an early age. Some have not gotten married until age 25 or 26 or 30, and some at age 17 or 18 or 20, but they have all been intentional. They have prepared themselves to be a husband, to be a provider, and to be a leader and protector. Their view of women stems from the Bible itself—a view that cherishes, upholds, serves, protects, and loves all women. We must challenge men to have courage, integrity, and the ability to lead. Who cares if the culture disagrees with us! We must be men who have iron chests.

These types of men are setting the standard for what dating/courtship (whatever you want to call it) looks like. These men are changing the way marriage should be viewed by young people. Again, it stems from a high view of the gospel. Marriage is indeed an illustration of Christ and the Church. Read Ephesians 5 over and over.

When men in the church pursue intentional preparation to be husbands early in life, they are setting the new standard of how marriage should be viewed—a biblical, gospel-centered standard—a standard that says marriage is just as important, if not more important, than success, money, and even… college.

Why Young Women Are Desiring to Be Wives & Moms First

ALLOW ME TO restate my conclusions above: Young men should prepare for and desire marriage at an early age to avoid sexual temptation, grow up early, become leaders, providers, protectors, and not be children at the age of 30. Also, I have not so arrogantly assumed that all bachelors in their 30's are children; I know a wide range of men who I admire, look up to, and are heroes of mine that are not married and are out of their 20's. A mentor of mine, who I also consider a hero, is in his later stages of life and is not married. Does this make him a child? For goodness sakes, absolutely not!

The issue here is intentional early preparation.

Now, with my conclusions well stated, I have given some thought to why so many young Christian women are desiring to forgo jobs and careers to be wives and moms who stay at home with their children.

With the rise of the feministic movement, traditional perspective on culture, family, law, politics, and human life have all been questioned and in most instances changed. The term feminism entered common parlance around the 1970s, though there were instances in previous years where the term was also used (i.e., Katherine Hepburn spoke of the 'feminist movement' in the year 1942 in her movie *Woman of the Year*). Forty years ago, the norm for women in the West was to stay at home, be moms, cooks, and housewives. Today, being a stay-at-home mom and a housewife is frowned upon and derided. Today, women will forgo just about anything to have careers. They will work long hours, send their kids to daycare, and travel all over the world, often at the neglect of their husbands, children, and homes.[2]

I have seen a trend amongst young Christian women who desire to be nothing but wives and moms. Yes, they want to finish their college education. Yes, they would like to obtain positions of service in the local church. Yet their primary motives for why they are alive is 1) to be a godly Proverbs 31 wife and 2) to be a caring, loving, and nurturing mother to their children.

Here are my thoughts on why this is an increasing trend.

---

[2]In my opinion, men are often more inclined to work long hours and neglect their families; also, I am not advocating that women be stay at home moms; my mother is one of the hardest working women that I have ever known (working full-time and going to school full-time during the evenings while she was pregnant with me, and had (has) an awesome marriage to my father all the while this was taking place). In the early stages of my life, I did attend daycare for a time (if I wasn't kicked out for being so bad – I was a biter), and all the while my mom was still a fantastic mother who fulfilled her role as a wife, mom and career woman.

1. Early Preparation.

AS I HAVE stated above, men and women should prepare themselves for marriage at an early age. This does not mean that they have to bypass careers to do so. Though this does mean that marriage should be the highest priority, even above college. The marriage relationship lasts much longer and reflects something so much greater than a college degree—Christ and his Church.

2. Early preparation is often found side-by-side with intentional parents.

THIS GENERATION is full of young men and women who want nothing more than four years of party-hard, crazy-drunk, get-naked college. Honestly, if that college existed when I was seventeen and thinking about college, then I would've been the first to sign up! Thankfully, Jesus saved me, which led me to stop seeing girls as objects, making myself look somewhat presentable, and then I began asking girls out with a higher IQ than me.

It seems to me that parents who are intentional about discipling their children and teaching them from an early age how to live with a biblical worldview often have children who are more mature earlier in life. It is in these Christian homes that young men and women are being trained and equipped to be husbands and wives early, rather than later. Most young men and women these days can't even spell marriage until they wake up from their thousandth hangover realizing they've been a senior for six years and realize they should probably start doing something productive with their lives. In my opinion, this is very sad, and reflects the cultural impact on American Christian families as well.

3. There are young Christian men today who care more about the pursuit of being married than money in their bank accounts, degrees on their walls, and cars in their garages.

THIS IS HOW YOUNG MEN are changing the world. Allow me to use myself as an example here. My girlfriend and I (who is now my wife) started dating when I was 21. I hadn't graduated from college yet. Eight months went by and then I proposed. Six months went by and we got hitched. I had just turned 23.

When I told people in my life that I wanted to get married at such an early age, and especially when I told them that my girlfriend and I had only been dating for eight months, almost everybody thought I was crazy. "Oh, you are so young," they would say. "Oh, but you're just a child," they would continue. "Oh, you've got plenty of time for that later," they would so confidently muster.

The difference between them and myself was that I was intentionally dating my girlfriend with marriage as the goal. I was not dating for recreational use. I wasn't just trying on another shoe to see if it would fit. I was intentionally preparing myself for marriage so that I would be a worthy husband for her.

Men, you don't need four years to figure out if she's "The One." As a pastor who I greatly admire often says, "You will find 'The One' standing right next to the unicorn."[3] Young Christian men are realizing this, growing up early, preparing themselves to be worthy husbands, and having courage to pursue relationships with girls by telling them on the first date that they want to intentionally pursue them with marriage in mind. The difference between recreational dating and intentional dating is that marriage is the purpose and goal towards which you are dating.

Men are realizing that they don't need to make lists of what they want in a girl; they are taking their lists, applying those characteristics to themselves, getting jobs, and actually paying for their dates instead of making their women pay for them. When young men become this kind of person they then attract young women who have been intentionally prepared by their daddies (and moms) to look for this type of guy and marry early.

4. Matters of Importance. Recapitulation.

THIS IS HOW YOUNG women are changing the world.

Today, young women are taking the heat of the

---

[3]Thank you Matt Chandler for this hilariously awesome phrase.

feminist word bombs and are saying that being a wife and mother is their primary calling.

We must be clear, it is no small task to be a wife and mother. Being a caregiver and a nurturer are amazingly great responsibilities, and also amazingly rewarding. With Scripture being their guide and the cultural norm at their backdoor, these women have decided that it is their responsibility to train the next generation for godliness. What ranks number one on matters of importance for these women is seeing their children know Jesus; training and equipping their children to know the Bible; making decisions using the filter of Scripture; living wisely according to that knowledge, even at an early age; developing a strong and foundational biblical worldview that will not be shaken; and preparing them to be leaders, providers, protectors, nurturers, affirmers, and caregivers.

I usually hate using the term "counter-cultural." As Christians we are called to engage culture and contextualize the gospel to the needs of culture. Shying away from culture oozes legalism and holy – art – thou – Christian – bubbles – that – nobody – cares – about. Though in this context, being counter-cultural is a positive thing, not negative a thing.

These young men and women are changing the view of marriage. Not within the culture. The world thinks we're crazy anyway. But within the evangelical church, young men and women are slowly changing their presuppositions concerning marriage.

This is something to get excited about. This is something that will last. This is something that will have an eternal impact.

What About Cohabitation Before Marriage?

ACCORDING TO A study done by *The National Marriage Project* (and affirmed by Focus on the Family research), an estimated half of all couples now cohabitate before they marry.[4] Also according to Focus on the Family, study after study has shown that couples who cohabitate before marriage are linked to poorer marital communication, lower marital satisfaction, higher levels of domestic violence, and a greater chance of divorce.

Young people will say and do just about anything to justify their actions in getting what they want… even if what they want is contradictory to what Scripture teaches. Young people have become so influenced by the culture that living together, even if one claims to be a Christian, is set outside of their so-called moral conscience.

They say, "It's okay if we live together because we are going to get married anyway." They continue, "We've been together for so long already it's like we are already married." And they continue, "We are just doing things backwards… it's no big deal." And they con-

[4]Amy Tracy, *Cohabitation as a Means to Marriage.* Focus on the Family. http://www.focusonthefamily.com/marriage/preparing_for_marriage/test_driving_marriage/cohabitation_as_a_means_of_marriage.aspx

tinue, "How do you know if you want to marry a person if you don't live with them first?" Those who say this and claim to follow Jesus have been blinded by their sin and are living a lie. They are not living according to the truth of Scripture.

We should refresh ourselves on what Scripture teaches concerning relationships, commitment, and marriage.

1. Cohabitation Leads to Fornication.

WHEN TWO PEOPLE live together who are incredibly attracted to one another, there is no way they can abstain from sex. Those who disagree are very naive and probably are continuing to find ways to justify their sin. Hebrews 13:4 says, "Let marriage be held in honor among all, and let the marriage bed be undefiled, for God will judge the sexually immoral and adulterous." Scripture continues, "Above all else, guard your heart, for it is the wellspring of life" (Proverbs 4:23). Cohabitation leads to fornication, which is a violation of Scripture. Also, we are called to guard our hearts until God has given us someone in which to cleave (Genensis 2). Living with someone defiles one of God's greatest gifts... marriage.

2. Cohabitation Rejects the Image of Christ & the Church.

WHEN COUPLES cohabitate it leads to a complete rejection of the relationship between Christ and the Church. The institute of marriage was given to us for two reasons: 1) reproduction—"Multiply and fill the earth"; and 2) it's an illustration of something greater—Christ and the Church.[5] In Ephesians 5:22-33, Paul gives us the example of Christ and the Church and relates it to how husbands and wives are supposed to live in relation to one another.

Men are supposed to present their wives as holy and blameless, without stain or wrinkle, or any other blemish. When couples cohabitate this presentation is marred. Men do not present their women as holy and blameless and pure; they are defiled and presented with stain and blemish. Men should strive to be men who love their wives as Christ loved his Church

3. Cohabitation Downplays Commitment.

WHEN COUPLES cohabitate they get everything they want in a relationship *now*, without the commitment of marriage *later*. Men get sex and women get marital intimacy—again, all outside of the commitment of marriage. According to the article cited above, by Amy Tracy of Focus on the Family,

---

[5]A third can also be stated, which is to glorify God.

"Young people today are cynical concerning the validity and longevity of the marital union. Indeed, with fifty percent of all marriages ending in divorce, men and women believe it's a good idea to try out different partners."[6] According to a 2002 report issued by the Center for Disease Control and Prevention's National Center for Health Statistics, the probability of a first marriage ending in separation or divorce within 5 years is 20 percent while the probability of a premarital cohabitation breaking up within 5 years is 49 percent.[7] These percentages drastically increase over time.

It is almost as if dating is equivalent to shoe shopping. Young people date today as if they are simply trying on different pairs of shoes. What young people don't understand, however, is that they are adopting a consumer mentality that is undercutting the fidelity of marriage. This is opening themselves up to marital breakup and unhappiness.[8]

The reason that so many marriages of those who cohabitate get divorced is the simple lack of commitment. When two Christians get married, they commit before God, themselves, and their witnesses that they will never get a divorce. Marriage has become the Cadillac of relationships for young people today. They want everything immediately. They want the perfect relationship. They want the intimacy. They want the

---

[6]Ibid.
[7]Ibid.
[8]Ibid.

sexual fulfillment. They want the house. They want the income. Today young people are getting all of this without the commitment of marriage, and they are becoming habituated to starting intimate relationships, breaking up, and then starting over. It is reflecting this consumer mentality to relationships, dating, and marriage, and it is failing to prepare them for a lifelong relationship.[9]

A Heed to Christians Who Live Together

THE GOOD THING about our God is that he is good, loving, and forgiving. When believers fall into sin, no matter the sin, God's grace is sufficient to forgive through the blood of Jesus. In fact, for the believer, *the blood of Jesus has covered all sin.* What a marvelous truth!

I would encourage Christians who live together to repent of their sin and move out! It's that easy. There is no room in a Scriptural view of marriage, relationships, and commitment, for cohabitation. I would encourage men to serve their women by beginning to present them in holiness and purity before God and honor them before their marriage.

---

[9]Ibid.

Dating, Courtship, & Wimpy Men Why the Current Dating Culture Must Change

LET'S GET RIGHT to it on this topic. The way young people date today pretty much reflects how married people relate to each other. Young people spend lots of time together alone; they awaken desire prematurely; they mess around, often times ending in intercourse; and they are just as affectionate as a husband and wife should be within the sacred confines of marriage. Most of the time, the only thing that separates a *dating* relationship from a *marriage* relationship is the ring that is parked on the left hand. Vodie Baucham says, as stated above, that dating as it is currently done is "glorified divorce practice." So, it's not hidden—I am a huge enemy toward the way we currently practice dating.

The difference between a Christian and a non-Christian when it comes to relationships should be monumental. For the Christian, the lens through which we view relationships must be Scripture. For the non-Christian, the lens through which they view relationships is often the current cultural approach. This approach is found in the saying, "You don't know if the shoe fits until you try it on." Men and women live with each other, fulfill their sexual desires, hop around from dating partner to dating partner, and treat each other as husband and wife—all without any form of commitment. Again, it is not uncommon to find confessing Christians living together before marriage either. If they are not living together it seems that they spend all of their time together in intimate environments where there is no accountability, and they have no one walking beside them as they pursue the biggest journey of their life.

The dating relationships of Christians must be different than those of non-Christians. Men, what does it say about you when you do not protect your girlfriend physically, emotionally, or mentally? Do you use the words, "I love you," without thinking twice about it as if love is really an emotion, and then when you aren't "feeling it" anymore you can just use the "it's not you, it's me" line? Oh man, there is nothing worse than a guy who uses a girl and then moves on to the next after he's gotten his fix! Do you often put yourselves in situations where temptation can be sparked? Have you awakened desire and intimacy before it is ready? If you can answer *yes* to any of these questions then you need to repent of your stupidity, and really begin to think about how you are forever hurting your sisters in Christ. Believe me guys; I've been there. I have done the things mentioned above, and thankfully God has shown grace upon me through his Son Jesus where I have had to repent of sin and become intentional about how I treat my sisters in Christ.

The way young people currently practice dating is killing not only their spiritual lives but it is killing the vitality of the church. This must change in our generation! Scripture does not necessarily say, "This is how you are supposed to date," but it does give us insights and wisdom into how men and women outside of marriage should relate to one another. Let's begin in Genesis 2. Genesis 2:24-25 says, "*Therefore a man shall leave his father and his mother and hold fast to his wife, and shall become one flesh. And the man and his wife were both naked and were not ashamed.*"

The Bible does not say that a man shall leave his father and mother and hold fast to his girlfriend. Let me be clear men, we don't join with our fiancées either. We join together with our wives. This is what is known as leaving and cleaving. Men, we leave our mother and father and we cleave to our wives. And obviously, we don't get naked with our girlfriends either. Do you ever wonder why you feel ashamed when you do?

So, if marriage is the end goal then what are the steps to getting there? Here's what I think, and honestly, it's this simple:

If you find yourself being sexually tempted then it's time to begin to prepare yourself for marriage (1 Corinthians 7:1-3). I realize that many people will disagree with me on this point, but that's okay, often times the ones who disagree with this are the ones who are justifying their actions of finding sexual pleasures outside of marriage—whether it's through sexual relationships or pornography. It has been said somewhere that 98% of men lust after women; the other 2% who say they don't lust after women are liars.

Young guys, you must have someone walk with you

through the dating/courtship process (Titus 2:1-10). I often tell young guys who ask me about courtship that it is simply the season of life when you are preparing yourself for marriage. If we are modeling discipleship/mentorship biblically then we should have an older man who is teaching and walking beside younger men as they make decisions. This includes their dating/courtship decisions.

Keep your dating/courtship/engagement time short (Song of Solomon 2:8; 8:4). Please don't date for five years before you get married. Seriously, is there any biblical wisdom in this? Let me tell you what will happen if you don't know already. You will be putting yourselves in five years of sexual temptation, desire, and struggle. Desire and love will awaken before its time. Also, when it comes to the engagement process then keep it as SHORT as possible. Believe me, this is the absolute WORST time for guys.

Begin to read books on marriage and not books on dating. Why would you want to read a how-to-guide on dating if you're only going to date for 6-8 months when you're going to be married for the rest of your life? Prepare yourselves to be husbands and wives, not boyfriends and girlfriends. Believe me, six to eight months is enough time for you to know if you want to spend the rest of your life with someone. You don't need a year to figure out if you want to see them naked or not, if you are like-minded, and if he or she loves Jesus. In all honesty, these are the only three requirements you must have to be compatible as husband and wife: 1) Do they love Jesus? 2) Are you attracted to them physically? 3) Are you like-minded in life, family, children, church affiliation, goals, etc.?

With that said, I implore you to begin to rethink your current dating situation if you are indeed in one that I have spoken of above. Let us be men who take the Bible seriously. Let us see the culture through the lens of Scripture—not vice-versa. I challenge you to be courageous in your dating, engagement process, and marriage.

Men, we must step up!

Let no one despise you for your youth, but set the believers an example in speech, in conduct, in love, in faith, in purity. Until I come, devote yourself to the public reading of Scripture, to exhortation, to teaching."
PAUL, *1 Timothy 4:12-13*

—CHAPTER FIVE—

LEARNING TO BE A LEADER

Please, No More Wimpy, Lazy, and Passive Men!

I LEARNED TO BE a leader on the basketball court. It was tough because I was really bad at it. I didn't understand the ends and outs of how to lead. I was pushy, bossy, and self-absorbed. I was out for myself. I wanted my stats, often at the expense of the team. Growing up, I was always the best player on any team I was a part of. Everybody looked for me to lead, however, again, I burned more bridges than I built. Throughout high school, I was so self-absorbed that I couldn't possibly lead well. I was the captain of the varsity basketball team my last two years, though again, I was captain ego. I remember my college basketball coach sitting me down one day and telling me that I could be a great leader if I ever learned to put others before myself. It was a devastating conversation to the ego I had built for myself. I will never forget that conversation. I have learned much about leadership over the years by simply remembering how bad of a leader I have been. Basketball indeed has taught me much over the years.

I have also been around several bad leaders in my life. I have learned more about how not to lead, or what not to do, around these types of leaders than anything else. Observing someone in leadership will teach you volumes about what to do and what not to do. It seems this type of observation has marked my life.

What is more, by God's blessing, I have been around some really great leaders over the past several years. I have had some great basketball coaches, great pastors, great mentors, great teachers, and a really great father whom all have taught me several different things about leadership.

All of these experiences, coupled with some intentional study of Scripture, and multiplied by learning the practitioner side of leadership, have all developed me into the leader I am today. I am still learning, however, to be a leader. I am still learning the practitioner and theological side of it. I am still learning how to be more like Jesus in my leadership. I am still learning how to put others before me by practicing servant leadership. I am still learning how not to be passive and lazy. I am still learning the negative effects of being a wimpy man. I am still learning it all!

Let me start off, however, by saying that this is not a how-to chapter on leadership. It is not my intention to give you a ten-step guide on being a leader. There are many great books for you to dive into on this subject already, and I have listed many of these books at the end of this chapter. It is my intention, though, to challenge you and maybe get under your skin a little bit. If you are a man who is passive, weak, lazy, unable to make decisions, stepped upon, bossed around, or unreliable, then this chapter is aimed at you. The church does not need passive men. The church does not need men who are weak. The church needs men who are leaders.

Our culture loves to portray men as lazy, overweight, bald, stupid, and idiotic. For instance, when I think of most TV shows this is the picture that comes into my head. It is usually a white man, though sometimes a black man, but NEVER a woman. Men get tossed around, stepped upon, and portrayed as morons by their wives and kids.

This chapter and the two succeeding chapters will discuss the characteristics of men being leaders, providers, and protectors. As men, we have a responsibility to benevolently lead, provide for, and protect women and children, according to the differing relationships we have with them.

The following is a theological plea for men to be leaders.

A Biblical Theology of Leadership in the Home & Church

WHO SHOULD LEAD in the local church? Who should lead in the family? How should we view leadership in respect to man's sinfulness? How should we view the mandate of leadership, given by God to his image-bearers, to be institutionalized throughout redemptive history, within the church and nuclear family? These are all questions that Scripture addresses. When looking at Scripture from cover to cover it becomes clear that leadership is something God is very passionate about. From the Garden to the New Jerusalem, God progressively unfolds characteristics, moral standards, and qualifications of what a leader is and ought to be. Concerning a biblical theology of leadership, we must look at the different stages of redemptive history (e.g., creation, fall, redemption, and new creation) and see the big picture of what Scripture says concerning specifically the *home* and the *church*.

Richard Lints says this about *redemptive history*,

> A fundamental fact about the Scriptures is that they constitute a text with a developing story. It is a story that clearly progresses toward the accomplishment of specific goals. Redemption is an activity of God that unfolds over time. This unfolding movement in the biblical text is profoundly important to the accomplishment of its purposes. We must remember that Scripture not only witnesses to God's re-

> demption but it is also an effective agent of that redemption. Biblical revelation progresses because it mirrors the progressive nature of redemption. The 'story' of God's involvement with and redemption of his people is acted out on the stage of history with many distinct but related parts.[1]

These related parts of the developing story of Scripture are broken down into four segments: creation, fall, redemption, and new creation. This progression of God's redemptive plan through these four stages of human history must be seen individually in how God works within the Trinitarian relationship. In reading Scripture Christocentrically,[2] we come to learn that the hero of the Bible is Jesus; the Father is summing up all things in Jesus; and Jesus will hand the finished and complete creation back over to the Father, giving the Father all the glory that is due his name. Redemptive history tells the story of the Father's plan for his creation through the complete exaltation of the Son. But what does redemptive history (human history recorded in Scripture) tell us about leadership?

Leadership in the Old Testament Family: Creation & Fall (Genesis 1-3)

"IN THE BEGINNING God created the heavens and the

---

[1]Lints, Richard, *The Fabric of Theology: A Prolegomenon to Evangelical Theology* (Grand Rapids, MI: Eerdmans Publishing Co., 1993), 262-63.

[2]Chirstocentric simply means "Christ-centered." When we view the entire Bible through the lens of Jesus then we begin to see how every verse in unity points to him!

earth."[3] Before God spoke creation into existence,[4] God has always existed in the ontological Trinity. Ontology is simply the nature of being or existing. God has always existed; he has always had being.[5] When looking only at Genesis 1-3, we see a few things:

1) God said, "Let *us* make man in *our* image and *our* likeness."[6] Not until a few thousand years of progressive revelation do we see who this *us* and *our* are in Genesis 1:26. Through a Christ-centered lens of Scripture, we find that the Father, Son, and Holy Spirit are all present in creation.

Colossians 1:15-20, John 1:1-18, and Hebrews 1:1-3 all give clarity to who God is speaking of in this verse. Bruce Ware rightly says, "It becomes clear that the work of God (e.g., creation, redemption, and consummation) can be rightly understood only as the work of the Father, Son, and Holy Spirit unified in the purpose of the work but distinct in the participation and contribution of each member."[7]

It is important to note that this Trinitarian relationship gives objectivity to how we view gender roles for men and women. Within the relationship of the Trinity we begin to see specific headship, as the Father (1

---

[3]Genesis 1:1

[4]Hebrews 11:3

[5]Men, we must learn big words. Let us be ashamed of ourselves if the largest word we know is a name printed on the back of a jersey.

[6]Genesis 1:26

[7]Ware, Bruce. *Father, Son, and Holy Spirit: Relationships, Roles, and Relevance* (Wheaton, IL: Crossway Books, 2005), 16-17.

Corinthians 11:3) is in authority over Christ.[8]

2) God gave Adam the mandate to "be fruitful and multiply, and fill the earth, and subdue it."[9] This text does not speak specifically to the details of how this would come about, only that there is a hint of a certain order to humanity and the continued existence of it. In the Garden, Adam is to be the primary leader; Adam was the one whom the mandate to cultivate the earth was given; Adam was the one who was given dominion over all the animals, fish, and birds; Adam was the one who was chosen to name the animals; and Adam was the one for whom Eve was made.

3) God made Eve as a "helper suitable for Adam," and Adam named the woman. Matthew Henry, a great theologian, said this about Eve being made as a helpmeet for Adam, "Power over the creatures was given to man, and as a proof of this he named them all. It also shows his insight into the works of God. But though he was lord of the creatures, yet nothing in this world was a helpmeet for man. From God are all our helpers."[10] It is important to note that the theme of leadership is present with Adam in the fact that Eve was created to be his helper even before sin was in the world. Also, the fact that Adam named Eve gives us the understanding that Adam is indeed the leader in the first marriage union.

---

[8]Piper, John and Wayne Grudem. *Recovering Biblical Manhood & Womanhood: A Response to Evangelical Feminism* (Wheaton, IL: Crossway Books, 2006), 137.

[9]Genesis 1:28

[10]Henry, Matthew. *Matthew Henry's Concise Commentary on the Whole Bible* (Nashville, TN: Thomas Nelson Publishers, 1997), 5.

4) God gave man the mandate to "leave his father and his mother, and be joined to his wife."[11] In large part, today's family fails to truly practice this leaving and cleaving concept, and in doing so, fails to fully understand and practice God's plan for the family. The biblical concept of leaving and cleaving gives implicit leadership implication for the man to be able and ready to cleave to his wife, not to mention leaving the umbrella of his parents.

What the Bible does not say is that boyfriends should leave their father and mother and cleave to their girlfriends. We join with our wives. This is *leaving* and *cleaving*. Men, we leave our father and mother to cleave to our wives—not our girlfriends, and not our fiancées either. And again, we don't get naked with our girlfriends. This can't be stated enough. There is a major cultural trend currently taking place, even amongst Christians, that they are cohabitating together before marriage. We will discuss this topic in detail later in this chapter.

5) Adam sinned by substituting himself in the place of the LORD, and the LORD "called Adam out" for his sin (Genesis 3). When Adam and Eve sinned, it was Adam whom the LORD pursued and held accountable. We again see a leadership theme given to Adam in that God held him accountable and not the woman. It is crucial to understand that this theme of leadership given to the man within the family, even

[11] Genesis 2:24

amidst the fall of humanity, continues to build as Scripture progresses.

6) God told Adam that his creation-mandated work will now be *hard* creation-mandated work; Adam will now work by the "sweat of his brow."[12] Instead of having anything he wants to eat in the Garden, Adam will now have to work for his food and work hard to be able to provide for his family. Again, leadership is given to Adam, even under the curse of sin.

7) God told the woman he will "greatly multiply her pain in childbirth" and that "her desire shall be for her husband."[13] This curse of the fall can be seen in homes all over the world throughout history, and more recently and specifically in a current postmodern movement called Evangelical Feminism. Wayne Grudem writes in his book *Evangelical Feminism*,

> This is a movement that claims there are no unique leadership roles for men in marriage or in the church. According to evangelical feminism, there is no leadership role in marriage that belongs to the husband simply because he is the husband, but leadership is to be shared between husband and wife according to their gifts and desires.
>
> And there are no leadership roles in the church reserved for men, but women as well as men can be

---

[12]Genesis 3:19

[13]Genesis 3:16. "In this context and in this construction, this word "desire" probably implies an aggressive desire, perhaps a desire to conquer or rule over, or else an urge or impulse to oppose her husband to act "against" him" (Grudem, Recovering Biblical Manhood and Womanhood, 33). This word for desire is used only in this way throughout all of the books of Moses.

pastors and elders and hold any office in the church.[14]

Evangelical feminists' attempt to disregard and find loopholes (i.e., reader response hermeneutics, literary/historical criticism, etc,) in God's mandate for the man to be the leader in the home and church, which can be traced all the way back to Adam's sin and the newfound curse for the woman.

8) God gives us the first gospel promise in that through the seed of the woman the serpent shall be defeated.[15] Though sin has now entered the world, marring and disrupting God's design for his creation, the LORD gives the first promise of redemption. We see the first of God's many promises planted here as he promises Eve that through her offspring he will crush the head of the serpent that deceived them. We see this promise fulfilled in the Warrior King Jesus Christ, who crushes the head of the serpent as he humbly and obediently becomes the penal substitutionary atonement[16] for the sin of his church.

There is a lot that takes place in the first three chapters of Genesis that clarify God's created order between men and women and their specific and biblically-defined gender roles.

---

[14]Grudem, Wayne. *Evangelical Feminism: A New Path to Liberalism?* (Wheaton, IL: Crossway Books, 2006), 1.

[15]Genesis 3:15

[16]Penal Substitutionary Atonement simply means that Christ died on a cross as a substitute for sinners. Jesus took the penalty for our sin. In doing so, God's wrath was applied to his Son, Jesus, instead of us. This was full payment for our sins. Hallelujah!

There are many more examples of leadership in the Old Testament that space will not allow here, but remember though, this is not a how-to-guide or a look – at – all – these – great – leaders – chapter. It is, on the other hand, an intentional look at how the Bible defines leadership and what the leader is supposed to be within the *family* and in the *church.* So, what does the Bible say about leadership in the New Testament church?

Leadership in the New Testament Church: Redemption and New Creation

IN LOOKING throughout the salvation-historical stages of redemption and new creation, it is important to look at certain passages that discuss qualifications and characteristics of leadership for the family and church. As God's redemptive revelation has progressed, we have now seen that Jesus has come as the greater David and has established his eternal Kingdom. Throughout the Old Testament we see leaders rise and fall under Gods ultimate leadership. The three main leadership offices in the Old Testament are Prophet, Priest, and King. Now that Jesus has come in the flesh, we see that he has fulfilled each of these three Old Testament offices in completeness. Jesus is the true prophet, priest, and king.

Also in the New Testament, we see a new institution established by Jesus—his church. As we have already seen that man is the authority and head of the family, it is not uncommon to think that Jesus would establish the man as the head of the household of God as well.[17] Now, as we look throughout the New Testament at what a leader is supposed to be, we will examine a few specific texts.

Acts 1-2

BEGINNING IN ACTS 1, we see Jesus promising his apostles the gift of the Holy Spirit before he bodily ascends into heaven. It is important to note that the apostles Jesus chose to lead his church were in fact men, the foundation for New Testament church leadership. When the apostles casted lots at the end of chapter 1 to see who would take Judas' place as the 12th apostle, Matthias, a man, was chosen. In Acts 2:2, we see that the Holy Spirit descended onto the apostles, and they began speaking in the tongues of those who were present. Reading on, we come to find out that Peter began to preach the gospel of the risen Lord Jesus to all those who were present. Scripture says that three thousand were added to their numbers that day. As we will see in 1 Timothy 3, Titus 2, and 1 Peter 5, one of the main qualifications for the pastor/elder in the church is for the leader to be a man.

---

[17] Strauch, Alexander. *Biblical Eldership: An Urgent Call to Restore Biblical Church Leadership* (Littleton, CO: Lewis & Roth Publishers, 1995), 58.

1 Timothy 3:1-7

THIS PASSAGE of Scripture is crucial for understanding the qualification of an elder/overseer. 1 Timothy 3:1-7 reads,

> It is a trustworthy statement: if any man aspires to the office of overseer, it is a fine work he desires to do. An overseer, then, must be above reproach, the husband of one wife, temperate, prudent, respectable, hospitable, able to teach, not addicted to wine or pugnacious, but gentle, peaceable, free from love of money. He must be one who manages his own household well, keeping his children under control with all dignity (but if a man does not know how to manage his own household, how will he take care of the church of God?), and not a new convert, so that he will not become conceited and fall into the condemnation incurred by the devil. And he must have a good reputation with those outside the church, so that he will not fall into reproach and the snare of the devil.

Paul begins by stating first and foremost that the office of an overseer belongs to a man. We see in Genesis 2 and 1 Corinthians 11 that God made man the head of the woman due to the order of creation, and Paul tells us that the office of an overseer also belongs to the man. The evangelical feminist argument again states that there is no designed leader in the church and the family. Paul here states that if a *man* aspires to the office of an overseer, it is a fine work *he* desires for himself. Twice in one verse Paul refers to this office as a masculine office. Not only does Paul define the office with a masculine pronoun but he also discusses the office holder of this office being a *husband*. For the third time in two verses, Paul discusses the qualifications of the overseer as a male.[18]

Titus 2:5-9

IN HIS LETTER to Titus, Paul gives the qualities and qualifications to look for in an elder. He says in Titus 2:5-9,

> For this reason I left you in Crete, that you would set in order what remains and appoint elders in every city as I directed you, namely, if any man is above reproach, the husband of one wife, having children who believe not accused of dissipation or rebellion. For the overseer must be above reproach as God's steward, not self-willed, not quick-tempered, not addicted to wine, not pugnacious, not fond of sordid gain, but hospitable, loving what is good, sensible, just, devout, self-controlled, holding fast the faithful word which is an accordance with the teaching, so that he will be able both to exhort in sound doctrine and to refute those who contradict.

[18]The office of *elder* is different than the office of *deacon*, which is a servant of the church. After prescribing the qualifications for the office of the elder, Paul then prescribes the qualification for the office of the deacon. Even within the complementarian position there are different views on whether or not a woman can serve as a deacon. For limited space, I will not even attempt this now. See the resource list at the end of this book.

Paul again defines the first quality of an overseer as a *man* saying, "If any *man* is above reproach." The text here that Paul is giving is strictly prescriptive as Paul lays out not only what an elder is supposed to be, but also what an elder is not supposed to be. When it comes to the office of the elder in the church, it is clearly defined for the man. We are to remember that men and women are in every way equal in dignity, value, and worth, but they are distinct in gender roles and function. John Piper writes, "Over the years I have come to see from Scripture and from life that manhood and womanhood are the beautiful handiwork of a good and loving God. He designed our differences and they are profound. They are not mere physiological prerequisites for sexual union. They go to the root of our personhood."[19]

For bible-believing Christians, the foundational argument for male leadership is found in the personhood of Jesus Christ, as found in the authoritative and infallible Scriptures. Scripture tells us that Jesus Christ is the Son of God, not the daughter of God. Alexander Strauch says this about Christ's personhood,

> It was a theological necessity, absolutely essential to his person and work. Jesus was and had to be a first-born male, "holy to the Lord" (Luke 2:23). As the "last Adam" and "the second man," He was the anti-type of Adam, not Eve. Therefore, he had to be male (1 Cor. 15:45, 47; Rom. 5:14). He had to be a

---

[19]Piper, John and Wayne Grudem. *Recovering Biblical Manhood & Womanhood: A Response to Evangelical Feminism*, 32.

> first-born son of David and Abraham, the true son of promise—the King, not the queen, of Israel and the Lord, not the lady, of the universe. According to the creation order, Jesus could not be a woman because in the male-female relationship the male partner alone is invested with the headship-authority role (Gen. 2:20, 22, 23; 1 Cor. 11:3; 1 Tim. 2:12), and Jesus Christ alone is Head of the Church and King of kings. He is the model for every male leader.[20]

Again, it is crucial to understand the manhood in the person of Jesus Christ and the model that he set forth for male leadership in the New Testament churches.

1 Peter 5:5

"YOU YOUNGER MEN, likewise be subject to your elders." Again, in this verse Paul discusses the office of an overseer as an office for a man. Some might say, "The elders here could be women that the young men are being subject to." That statement is not likely when you follow the rule of interpreting Scripture with Scripture. Following a Titus 2 model, Paul tells the younger men to learn from their elders (older men). In Titus 2, Paul tells the older men to teach the younger men to learn the duties of the church and the maturity

---

[20]Strauch, Alexander. *Biblical Eldership: An Urgent Call to Restore Biblical Church Leadership,* 58-59.

of the faith. It is crucial to understand that the only time the office of an elder is spoken of in the New Testament it is talked about under male leadership.

We must conclude that the office of the New Testament overseer must be paralleled to the person of Jesus, the choosing of the 12 apostles, the qualifications given by Paul and Peter, and the creation mandate of the man as the leader of the family. The New Testament leader for the office of the pastor/elder must be a man.[21]

Leadership in the New Testament Family: Redemption and New Creation

SCRIPTURE GIVES clear definitions on defined gender roles for the husband and the wife. The most obvious reference to the husband and wife in the New Testament is Ephesians 5. Ephesians 5 is worth quoting in full as it reads,

> Wives, submit to your husbands as to the Lord. For the husband is the head of the wife as Christ is the head of the church, his body, of which he is the Savior. Now as the church submits to Christ, so also wives should submit to their husbands in everything. Husbands, love your wives, just as Christ loved the church and gave himself up for her to

[21] Evangelical Feminists will also bring up the argument that Paul's qualifications for the office of elder were only cultural and should not be applied to the life of the church today. Again, for space I will not tackle this now but this is by far the most amusing argument that people (mostly power-hungry females) give for stating their view on this. See resources at the end of this book for further study. I am also differentiating between elders and deacons. It is my conviction that deacons can be both men and women if they are properly functioning as servants of the local church.

> make her holy, cleansing her by the washing with water through the word, and to present her to himself as a radiant church, without stain or wrinkle or any other blemish, but holy and blameless. In this same way, husbands ought to love their wives as their own bodies. He who loves his wife loves himself. After all, no one ever hated his own body, but he feeds and cares for it, just as Christ does the church— for we are members of his body. 'For this reason a man will leave his father and mother and be united to his wife, and the two will become one flesh.' This is a profound mystery—but I am talking about Christ and the church. However, each one of you also must love his wife as he loves himself, and the wife must respect her husband.

Husbands are to *love* and *serve* their wives as Christ served the church. Paul discusses the authority/headship/leadership of the man as nothing less than Christocentrically.

Leadership must be servant leadership

PAUL DRAWS OUT the fact that Christ served his church and gave himself up for her. The husband must lead his wife this way. He must lead her to the point of giving himself up for her, even to the point of death. Often in the evangelical community, servant leadership is called *mature masculinity*, as we stated in the introduction. Let us quote John Piper again as he gives this definition of mature masculinity: "At the heart of mature masculinity is a sense of benevolent responsibility to lead, provide for, and protect women in ways appropriate to a man's differing relationships."[22]

What Leadership is and is Not

CONCERNING *LEADERSHIP* in our subculture of Evangelicalism, leadership is often taken to the extreme and can be very sinful, not to mention idiotic for the man. The call to lead the woman is not a hyper-leadership form of egotistical consumption, though it is a call to serve the woman. Questions to ask are, "What is best for her? What can she handle at one time? What would she like to do?" Yes, the man should assume his responsibility in undertaking the final say in disagreements, but he should not use this like a trump card. Leadership is humble, repentant, risk-taking, and sacrificial. Concerning *provision* for the woman, as we will see, this is often backwards thinking in our feminist and pseudo-intellectual society. The man should feel a great responsibility to provide for the woman, not that the woman should not assist in maintaining support for the family, but the man should feel a benevolent responsibility to always work hard, and do what he has to do to provide for his wife and family. Genesis 3:9 says, "But the Lord God called to the man and said to him, "Where are you?"[23] Concerning *protection* for the

---

[22]Piper, John and Wayne Grudem. *Recovering Biblical Manhood & Womanhood: A Response to Evangelical Feminism, 35-45.*

[23]Ibid.

woman, also as we will see, mature masculinity senses the natural urge to always protect the woman (any woman for that matter) from the context of danger by putting himself between an adversary and a woman. This is simply an understanding of mature masculinity where men should strive to be bold and courageous (Joshua 1).

Who goes into the lifeboats first when the ship is sinking?[24]

Concerning a biblical theology of leadership, we must start with the personhood of Jesus and work our way out from there. Jesus is the model for male leadership in the home and in the church. Modeling after Jesus in leadership has major implications in how one ethically presents himself according to biblical moral standards. Jesus was the second Adam, but the first true and perfect leader. He was what Adam (and all after Adam) could not be as a leader. Therefore, we must always model our leadership after the life of Jesus. After looking at the life of Jesus, we must look at what the rest of the New Testament says concerning the qualifications of leadership within the home and church. Paul and Peter give the leadership/authority/headship position to the man inside both the home and church, calling leaders to serve sacrificially as Christ served the church. Looking at Genesis 1-3, we understand that God gave specific leadership qualities to Adam, but Adam failed to complete this true leader-

---

[24]Ibid.

ship calling due to the sin of substituting himself for God. Only in Jesus do we find what true servant leadership is under the atoning sacrifice he made in substituting himself for us on the cross.

A Few Last Thoughts

WITH THAT SAID, here are a few things I want to get off my chest:

Men, we must lead boldly in the home and in the church. I will not go into this much more since I just gave a pretty hefty overview of why this should be the case according to the Bible. It kills me when men are not leaders in the home. When it comes to the church, we must begin to put aside this "Christianity is for the weak" mentality, and step up and serve where there is need. You don't have to be a pastor to serve or lead in the church. Ask your pastor where you can serve, if you are not already, and get your family involved as well. Every Christian family should be serving in his or her church.

Men, leadership is humble. Again, leadership is not an egotistical consumption of people serving you. Leadership is humble. People can see right through losers who think they are kings. Please, don't be that guy.

Men, leadership is sacrificial. We must mirror and reflect the most perfect leader—Jesus. Leadership is not dirty delegation where you are simply ordering people around. True leadership is servant leadership. We must serve others in order to effectively lead them.

Men, leaders are confident. There is a difference between confident and cocky, but in all honesty, most people can't tell the difference. A confident leader can take criticism because he is humble and sure of his abilities as he is leading others from point A to point B. A cocky leader thinks mostly of himself and when someone criticizes him he either gets really angry and loses his temper or he goes and cries in the closet. A confident leader does not need others to encourage him as he is leading others because he is confident himself, yet humble in his abilities to lead. A cocky leader wants people to praise his every move. Those guys should step into the octagon with a UFC fighter.

Men, leaders must have courage. Yes, we must have courage to step into the octagon, enlist in the military, or step onto a battlefield… no matter what the battle, but we must also have courage in how we present ourselves in our speech and action.

Men, look behind you and see who is following you. If no one is following you then you probably don't have a lot of influence as a leader. If this is the case then ask yourself where you might be able to step up and be a leader. What about your home? What about your church?

I am thankful for the men who have gone before me that have taught me these things. I am thankful for my dad, Jerry. I have thankful for my brothers Nathan and Chad. I am thankful for my father-in-law, George.

I am thankful for my brothers-in-law, Trent, Everett, Luke, Isaac, and Jonathan. I am thankful for my basketball coaches, David Ball, Casey Smallwood, and Corey Mullins. I am thankful for the mentor-pastors that have been in my life, Trent Stewart, Daniel Broyles, Brandon Shields, and Jon Akin. I am thankful for the men who sharpen me daily, Zack Thurman, Gabe Slone, Tyler Smith, Tyler Kesler, Whitney Clayton, and others I have not mentioned here. I am very thankful that God has put these men in my life for different seasons. What is more, I am very thankful that God is allowing me to continue to learn how to be a leader. I pray this chapter encourages you to do and be the same.

"... if anyone is not willing to work, let him not eat."
PAUL, *1 Thessalonians 3:1*

—CHAPTER SIX—

†

LEARNING TO BE A PROVIDER

Wearing the Big Boy Pants

IF ANYONE IS NOT willing to work, let him not eat. This is a pretty clear statement by Paul concerning idleness and laziness. Paul gives this clear and explicit statement to the church in Thessalonica right before his closing benediction. He commands us, his readers, to keep away from anybody who might be walking in this way. He then reminds his readers about the example he put forth in working hard and presenting himself in toil and labor: "For you yourselves know how you ought to imitate us, because we were not idle when we were with you, nor did we eat anyone's bread without paying for it, but with toil and labor we worked night and day, that we might not be a burden to any of you" (1 Thess. 3:6-8).

"But with toil and labor…"

THESE ARE TWO words that, at first glance, aren't rather welcoming. We are not born with an innate desire to toil and labor in our work. In other words, we are not, by nature, hard workers.

When I was a child, I was not a very hard worker. Like most kids, I hated doing chores around the house. I hated cleaning my room. I hated doing the dishes. I hated taking out the trash. But I loved to work hard at playing outside with friends. I loved to work hard at playing sports. I loved to work hard at trying to be cool. Most young boys don't have to be taught to enjoy the latter. School came natural to me so I really didn't have to work hard at that either. I had to learn to work hard in the areas of my life in which I didn't really enjoy working hard.

It helped, though, that I have a lot of hard workers in my family. My papaw is a blue-collar man who can do just about anything with his hands. He worked security at the University of Tennessee for the majority of his life. He raised my father on a farm where he experienced lots of early morning chores, mid-afternoon chores, after-dinner chores, and… a lot of hard work. In turn, my dad worked hard in school, and he became the valedictorian of his class. He went on to get an engineering degree from the University of Tennessee and a master's degree in business. He met my mom, who is also a very hard worker, married her and not soon thereafter had me. My mom, as I have mentioned elsewhere, was working full-time, going to school full-time, and keeping up with the home all while she was pregnant with me. While I do believe women can work and have extremely successful careers, I want to be clear: being the provider and working hard is a primary role for the man. I am a firm believer in a woman being a worker, having a career, and being successful, but I am absolutely convicted and certain that the man is supposed to be the primary provider for the entire family. Again, my father was this. He worked hard at everything he did. At one point when I was in school, my father was waking up at 4:00 AM for his job every single day. He has proven himself a hard worker, and he has become extremely successful as an engineer.

My father was also a hard worker at being a dad. I have tons of memories of him playing with my little brother and me in the back yard, throwing the ball around, shooting hoops, and just hanging out. He taught me how to mow the yard, trim, mulch, work with my hands around the house, treat women by how he taught me to treat my mom, be polite, and work hard myself. Obviously, as a young boy with a quick tongue, I definitely had my pushbacks. I had to *learn* to be a hard worker. It did not come easy. I also learned to work hard on the basketball court. I played ball all the way up through high school and even into college at two different schools. Basketball taught me that if you don't work hard in practice then you don't play in games.

In high school I got my first job working as a bagger at a local grocery store, or as I liked to call my title, "a courtesy clerk." I remember getting my first $20.00 tip for carrying an old lady's grocery bags out to her car. It was one of those ritzy grocery stores. I remembered how good it felt to be rewarded for hard work. As I got older, however, the work got more intense, but the rewards got even sweeter. I remember going up to my grandparents house and helping my grandfather put in a barbed-wire fence around his garden to keep out the cows. He paid me $200.00 for 2 days of work. The work was hard but the reward was sweet.

As I got to college I learned rather quickly that the work was even harder still. I didn't work hard my first semester at my first college, and I quickly realized the consequences. I slept through one of my finals and made straight C's for the first time in my life. I got home that summer and realized that I had better step up my game plan because the consequences for my current work ethic toward school was not going to cut it. I needed to buckle down and start getting after it.

It was also during this time where God really began to get a hold of my life and project my passions and desires toward full-time ministry. I struggled for a while with the calling, but after a while I knew that God was leading me to begin to study to be a pastor, or so I thought.

I got accepted to Boyce College in Louisville, KY the day that classes started, so we packed up my car and my parent's car and headed four and a half hours north.

This is where I learned about the biblical theology of hard work. I quickly began to realize that hard work is biblical and isn't just something my parents do for a living. I also began to learn why I had to *learn* to be a hard worker.

In the beginning of the book of Genesis, God calls Adam to be a worker. Genesis 1:26-28 says, "Then God said, 'Let us make man in our image, after our likeness, And let them have dominion over the fish of the sea and over the birds of the heavens and over the livestock and over all the earth and over every creeping thing that creeps on the earth.' So God created man in his own image, in the image of God he created him; male and female he created them. And God blessed them. And God said to them, 'Be fruitful and multiply and fill the earth and subdue it and have dominion over the fish of the sea and over the birds of the heavens and over every living thing that moves on the earth.'"

Before the fall, God called Adam to work the ground, cultivate it, subdue it, and have dominion over it. He was to work the ground, eat from it, and care for it. He was to make his area beautiful.[1] Have you ever seen someone's yard that has been cultivated and subdued? My father-in-law is a landscape architect. His yard looks like something out of a storybook. It is ab-

[1]Let us not mistake beautiful for a feminine word. Our hard work can and should be described as beautiful work.

solutely amazing. He takes the time to work hard, labor, cultivate, and have dominion over his yard. In the same way Adam was called to have this type of dominion over the Garden of Eden. In the exact same way, we are called to have dominion over similar areas of our lives, whether it is our yards or homes, being organized, disciplined, healthy, clean, or intentional in our hard work. This is our calling as men.

What we often forget is that work is biblical. What we often also forget is that toilsome work is the product of sin.

In Genesis 3, we see that the ground was cursed because of Adam's disobedience to God, the Father. Genesis 3:17-18 says, "And to Adam he said, 'Because you have listened to the voice of your wife and have eaten of the tree of which I commanded you, 'You shall not eat of it,' cursed is the ground because of you; in pain you shall eat of it all the days of your life; thorns and thistles it shall bring forth for you; and you shall eat the plants of the field. By the sweat of your face you shall eat bread, till you return to the ground, for out of it you were taken; for you are dust, and to dust you shall return."

It seems from this passage that sin, work, and death are now all related to each other. What once was good (work) has now become cursed (toilsome work through thorns and thistles). In each case though, Paul's statement that we have already quoted above still stands. Whoever does not work should not eat. Adam had to work to eat in the Garden of Eden, but now because of sin he must pursue toilsome work by the sweat of his brow to eat. Creation is now battling against our mandate to cultivate it. In Romans 8:19-22, we see that creation is groaning for men to cultivate it. After the fall, creation was subjected to frustration, making our work hard work. What's more, our calling as men to be "dominion takers" has now been marred by the fall. Sin has, therefore, affected both the status of work (now being hard) and our desire to do it (dominion rulers).

We can see the theological progression of *work* as follows:

- God created man (Genesis 1:26-27)
- He gave us the mandate to work (Genesis 1:28)
- Work would provide the way for Adam to eat (Genesis 1:29-30)
- Adam fell into sin (Genesis 3:6-7)
- God cursed the ground (Genesis 3:17-18)
- Adam's work (and our work through Adam) has now become toilsome (Genesis 3:19)
- Work is still the means that provides food, but now we eat through the sweat of our brow (Genesis 3:19)

The curse has turned the desire for work in men to the default setting of laziness, as mentioned above (1 Thessalonians 3:10-12)

Learning to Work Even Harder

I HONESTLY DIDN'T know what *hard work* meant until I combined being newly married with my second semester of full-time seminary. I met my wife, Grace, in Louisville, KY, where we went to school. We began to hang out through a mutual friend and it didn't take me long to notice how amazing this girl was. Throughout that second semester of college we hung out more and more, and I just knew that I wanted to date Grace with the intentions of marriage. And most of you will think I'm crazy for doing this, but I let my intentions be known from the get go. We were hanging out at a Starbucks in Louisville and I was about to leave to go to Seattle, WA for a conference. As we sat talking in the parking lot about to leave, I knew that I couldn't wait a week to let her know my intentions and how I felt about her. So, as we talked, I thought of the smoothest transition I could muster before I told her what I had wanted to tell her for the last few weeks. I'm not going to tell you the transition that I used because I don't want you to plagiarize it one day, but I will tell this… it was pretty awesome.

So as we talked, I let my intentions be known.

I said, "[insert transition here]" and then I said, "I would like to date you with the intentions of marriage."

I let her know from the get go that our dating relationship was going to be intentional. I was going to work hard at it... and so began the work ethic that I currently have today.

Grace and I dated for eight months, were engaged for five, and got married on April 18, 2009. I then began to understand what hard work really was... in a whole new way. The dating process took intentional hard work for it to be successful. The engagement process did the same. And marriage is no different.

Throughout seminary I began to work odd jobs here and there to provide for our small family that we had accumulated...Grace, my dog, and myself. At one point during seminary I was working three jobs for a grand total of about 55 hours or more a week. I was working as a server at a restaurant, a residential counselor at a local boys and girls home, and doing odd jobs around the city. And don't forget about seminary. Nine hours of classes is full time at that level of school, and I was doing 16-18 hours every semester. Don't ask me how I did it. God has given me a somewhat astonishing ability to do several things, at somewhat high levels, all at the same time. Maybe it's my personality combined with my ultra-heightened gift of administration. Whatever it is... I would suggest not trying to do that much if I were you. Working hard is one thing, but working hard at the expense of not being able to stop is another thing. I have repented much. I have failed a ton.

I also learned about taking care of my body and health during this time. I gained almost 25 pounds during seminary. I worked and worked and worked at the expense of my own health. I was young and my blood pressure was high. I wasn't over weight but I was still very unhealthy on the inside. God taught me a lot about working hard not only for the provision of my family but also for the health of my body. I now have little trouble working hard at being in shape, though again, at times I still fail. I also have little trouble at working hard at resting. Although I still struggle to put aside work, God is giving me a renewed sense of being still, having fun, and being intentional with my rest.

Working Hard At Many Things

A MAN IS A PROVIDER. I have told my wife several times that I will do whatever I have to do to provide for our family, even it means working 100 hours a week. I would hate it, but I would do it because, as a man, I am called to do it. I would encourage you to begin to think through this concept now. What areas of your life do you need to improve your work ethic? How are you not providing for your family?

Here are a few areas that I am constantly evaluating in myself to see if I need a gut check in work ethic. Hopefully they will help you too.

Work. I always ask myself, *am I working hard at work*? How do my co-workers see my work ethic? Am I being an example in my work ethic to the other men in my place of employment? What areas can I improve in my work ethic at work? We should always work hard at work. There are times for goofing off and there are times for work. I'm not a stickler but I do think we should always mind the time that we are getting paid for. This concept bleeds into the virtue of honesty. Is the work you are getting paid for honest work, or are you working half the time and goofing off the other half?

School. We don't often think about school being a place where we should point a good amount of work ethic. Are you working to do the very best you can, with the time and resources God has given you in the classroom? Whether you are in high school, college, or graduate school, you should always place a great effort toward making school a top priority.

Studying. This is another area that is often placed at the bottom of the list for men. We must work hard in applying ourselves to study. This is a discipline that must be practiced weekly, if not daily. What are you reading? What discipline are you working through currently? A Christian man must be a reading man. We must continuously equip ourselves to learn the entire counsel of God's Word (1 Timothy 3:16), as well as always be prepared in season and out of season to give an answer for anybody who might ask us for the reason for the hope that we have (1 Peter 3:15).

Relationships. Relationships don't come natural. Whether it is a dating/courtship relationship, a relationship with our parents or siblings, or a relationship with a friend, we must always work hard at keeping them healthy and Christ-centered. I have an inner circle of friends that I am constantly calling, emailing, and checking up on. I want to continue to work on the relationships I have with my inner circle of friends. They are that important to me. As iron sharpens iron, so one man sharpens another (Proverbs 27:17).

Marriage. This one really goes without saying. Like everything in life, you must work at something for it to be successful. Marriage is no different. I hope to one day write a book on the role of a man within marriage, what I have found to be the most challenging and helpful advice for newly-married couples on beginning this new life with your spouse. This relationship, however, is the single most rewarding relationship outside of a relationship with Jesus. Like everything in life, the work is hard, but the reward is so amazingly sweet.

Exercise. This is often a forgotten form of discipline. We are called as Christians to take care of our bodies and be good stewards over our health. I realize this might be outside of the genre of provision, but it is not outside of the discipline of hard work, which is what I understand the concept of being a provider to be. I would encourage you to find a good and reasonable workout plan and stick to it. Get someone to workout with you so you can both be accountable to taking care of yourself. I come from a Baptist background where we run from the mention of alcohol. I always thought this to be funny because the men who bash alcohol are often the same men who are extremely over weight and very unhealthy. What is worse for you? One glass of wine or a Big Mac with a large fry? Let us keep our priorities in line as men. A man who practices biblical manhood is a man that takes care of his body.

The Constant Pursuit of Biblical Manhood. We must never think we have arrived as men. We must always continue to lead a life of learning, evaluating, and repenting. We must *learn* to be men of courage; we must *learn* how to teach and defend the gospel; we must *learn* how to prepare ourselves for marriage; we must *learn* how to become a leader in our homes, churches, and places of influence; we must *learn* how to work hard and become a provider; and we will see in the next few chapters that we must *learn* to carry ourselves as protectors, be able to make good and quick decisions, and fight for holiness in everything we do. It is not easy. It takes hard work. But the reward is amazing! And when we do fail, our gracious God who has a perfect standard is quick to forgive us through the blood of Jesus Christ. Gospel-centered manhood allows us to examine our failures and successes in the light of an eternal perspective. This eternal perspective is God-centered. Therefore, when we fail, we rest in the gospel and go to the Father for forgiveness, and furthermore, when we succeed, we can always examine our success through the gospel as well. We are God's prized possessions whom he has given strength, energy, and specific skills—all of this applies to how we view the posture of working hard as men. We must work hard and give thanks.

My wife and I just had our second child. Some of you might read this and automatically disqualify me for writing a book on biblical manhood since I have not yet passed the *mature* threshold of fatherhood. I want you to remember though, this book is my journey into what a man is supposed to be, and these are my convictions on what we should teach our up-and-coming generations about what being a man truly is. We are still a little family. One day we might become a big family. I often sit and daydream about the big family that God might give my wife and me. I see us having several more children, biological and adopted.

But no matter how big God grows our little family, or if we stay the same as we are now, I can promise you this: I will work hard, labor hard, toil by the sweat of my brow hard, and *provide* for my family until my last breath. I will provide shelter, food, and clothing for my family. I will provide toys, random outings, vehicles, and fun vacations. I will provide healthy self-esteems, confidence in the Lord, and healthy goals to strive for. I will provide countless prayers, never-ending hugs, kisses, and continual and daily laughter. But most of all I will provide them with the gospel of Jesus Christ and place it at the center of everything we do as a family. For one day I will stand before my King and I will fall on my face and thank him with tears of joy for the earthly family he has given to me. I will then look around to see my heavenly family, the one he *provided* his life for, from every tribe, tongue, and nation gathered around his throne. And there I will rest with joy from my hard work—my successes and my failures. For my work will be done.

"At the heart of manhood is the benevolent responsibility to humbly lead, provide for, and [protect] women and children in ways appropriate to a man's differing relationships." JOHN PIPER

—CHAPTER SEVEN—

LEARNING TO BE A WARRIOR

The Forgotten Virtue of Being a Protector

WHEN I WAS IN elementary school I was a little wimp. I use to get picked on, called names, and ignored every day. I was a little scrawny kid. I wasn't shy or quiet, so that couldn't have been the reason I was picked on. I was actually pretty hyper. I was one of those kids that had to be put on medicine because I was so hyper. I wasn't the only one who got picked on though. I remember there was this girl in my class who was kind of different. She would get picked on as well and called names everyday by the boys in the class. To make things worse, I would join in on the game of name calling because I did not want to be the one getting picked on myself. I thought if I would join them and pick on her then they would forget about picking on me.

Wow, is my view of the female gender totally different now than it was when I was seven years old… and rightly so.

As I think over that scenario in my head, I wish I could go back to my little, skinny as a tooth pick, hyper as ever, seven-year-old body, apologize and stand up for her. If I knew and understood then what I know now, there would be some crazy seven-year-old fist-fights going down.

As I got older, I grew into my body and was always one of the most athletic boys in school. In middle school, I was one of the most popular kids in school because I was the best basketball player. I was athletic and beginning to understand that my muscles would continue to grow if I worked out from time to time, but I still failed miserably at understanding my role as a young man.

One day, just before a middle school basketball game, I was sitting with a bunch of friends watching the middle school girls team play before us. A girl was sitting below me on the bleachers and got up to tell a friend something. I slid into her seat before she could sit back down. This didn't make her happy at all. She tried to jam herself between me and the person sitting next to me. She then began yelling at me and slapping me in the face. After about the second slap I lost it and punched her in the nose.

Blood started gushing everywhere. Everybody just kind of gasped because of what just occurred. She ran to the bathroom crying, holding her nose, and everybody was just looking at me. It was definitely a low moment in my middle school career.

To make things worse, as she ran into the bathroom my mom was coming out and they met face to face. She told my mom what happened. My mom told my dad. My dad then whooped me later that night. And I apologized the next day.

I failed at being a protector that day in middle school. I will never forget that day.

When I got to high school, I often failed as well. I never have hit another girl since that awful day in middle school, but I began to fall short in protecting them again. I remember a time when I got into a verbal fight with a female ""friend" of mine. I began cursing at her and calling her names that I would be ashamed to even mention now. This verbal assault lasted months. Every time this particular girl would walk by me, I would go out of my way to assault her verbally. There were also times that I took advantage of girls because of my popularity in basketball. I look back on those days and it makes me sick to my stomach. What a failure at being a man I was at that time in my life.

I finally graduated high school and ventured into the realm of college. By his grace alone, God began to grow me spiritually, and I began reading my Bible more; and I began to pursue God's call on my life to vocational ministry. As I mentioned before, I moved to Louisville, KY, and I began to study the Scriptures pretty heavily.

I started taking serious the concept of being a protector when I starting dating Grace, who is now my wife. I knew I wanted to marry her so I began to read everything I could get my hands on concerning marriage, biblical manhood, and being a husband. I read John Piper's, *Recovering Biblical Manhood & Womanhood*, in like a week. I read Andreas Kostenberger's book, *God, Marriage, and Family*, like three times. I read Vodie Bauchum, Mark Driscoll, Stuart Scott (not the ESPN guy), Paul Tripp, James Dobson, Dave Harvey, and many others like them that champion the concept of biblical manhood and all that it entails. I talked to friends about this concept. I became obsessed with it.

I began to ask the question, "If we are called as men to be husbands, then what does this specifically entail?" And I kept coming back to three words: Leadership, Provision, and Protection.

Leadership, Provision, and Protection

THE FIRST TWO seemed to me to be pretty tangible and had the ability to bring immediate fruit from my efforts. The third though, the concept of protection, was harder for me to begin to put into practice. It wasn't hard because I didn't understand it; it was hard because I didn't see the immediate fruit of my labors concerning this ever-important truth. So I again began to study Scripture to understand how I was supposed to fulfill this role as being a protector. Here are a few important passages that speak to the concept of men being protectors of women and children.

1 Peter 3:7

"Likewise, husbands, live with your wives in an understanding way, showing honor to the woman as the weaker vessel, since they are heirs with you of the grace of life, so that your prayers may not be hindered."

MEN, WE ARE TO show honor to women in everything that we do. Peter exhorts us to live with her in an understanding way, showing *honor* to her. This word *honor* points to royalty and greatness. We are to honor our spouses with this great sense of worthiness. We are to cherish them. We are to hold them in high esteem above everything else. The description *weaker vessel* is not necessarily derogatory terminology either. To Peter, this description is beautiful. As men and women we are to understand the amazing differences that exist between us. God has created both men and women in his image and after his own likeness.[1] The concept of gender roles is extremely important. If women were to act as protectors then God would have undoubtedly made them bigger and stronger. As men, we must understand our role as the stronger vessel. We are not only to live with women in an understanding way when it comes to serving them and attempting to understand the beautiful complexities of womanhood, but we are

[1]Genesis 1:26.

to live as protectors toward women, realizing that God has created us for such a task. We must put ourselves in between harm and her. This is our calling and duty as men.

Ephesians 5:23 & 29

For the husband is the head of the wife even as Christ is the head of the church, his body, and is himself its Savior …For no one ever hated his own flesh, but nourishes and cherishes it, just as Christ does the church".

AGAIN, WHAT A beautiful truth! In this passage, Paul parallels the aspect of Christ being the head of the church with the husband being the head of Christ. I don't know if I have shared yet how thankful I am for my wife. She is a gem and a jewel to me. She is so encouraging. She is so sweet. She is so beautiful in my eyes. It is no secret… I am totally and absolutely in love with her. I am most thankful for the way my wife practices and models biblical womanhood. She allows me to be the spiritual leader of our home. She is so patient with me when I am not practicing the truths I have been writing about. She is always the first to forgive me for my shortcomings and failures. What an amazing woman she is.

As the head of my home, there is no greater challenge than to protect this little family that God has given me. I pray often that God would make me like Christ in this endeavor. The concept of being a protector is such an amazing picture of the gospel. Jesus substituted himself for us on the cross. He accomplished the defeat of sin, and he graciously applies his death to the elect, his ransomed church. Oh, until all the ransomed church of God be saved to sin no more! What a marvelous day that will be indeed. Until Jesus returns though, we as men have a great duty and responsibility before us. As we are one with our wives, we must nourish, cherish, and love them. As Paul says, "For no one ever hated his own flesh, but nourishes and cherishes it, just as Christ does the church." If we cherish our spouses then we will protect them at all cost. We will put ourselves between them and danger. And like Jesus, we would graciously give and sacrifice our own lives for them. As John Piper says, "Every wife knows that something is amiss in a man's manhood if he suggests that she get out of bed 50% of the time to see what the strange noise is downstairs."[2]

1 Timothy 5:8

"But if anyone does not provide for his relatives, and especially for members of his household, he has denied the faith and is worse than an unbeliever."

WE DISCUSSED THIS passage in the previous chapter on provision, but it is pertinent to this discussion, too. I can't get past the sternness of Paul's language here. If a man will not provide for his relatives, *especially for the*

---

[2]John Piper & Wayne Grudem, *Recovering Biblical Manhood & Womanhood: A Response to Evangelical Feminism* (Wheaton: Crossway, 2006), 43.

members of his own household, then that man has denied the faith and is worse than an unbeliever. There is a hint of failing at being a protector in this passage as well. As men, we are called to work,[3] and if we are not working we are not protecting women. It is the man who must work by the sweat of his brow to provide for his family, not the woman. It is our curse, passed down from Adam, and even though a curse, it is still our great duty.

There is also a hint of the man protecting not only his spouse in this passage, but also other women, appropriate to the differing relationships he has with them. If my sister was in trouble you better believe I would come to her rescue. If my friend's wife was in trouble you better believe I would do what I could, in an appropriate way, to help her. It is the duty of every man to walk with a cognitive sense of protecting all women and children from harm and danger, and as Paul states above, especially his own family.

A Personal Story About Putting My Scrawny Neck on the Line

WHEN MY WIFE and I were still living in Louisville, KY as I finished up seminary, we lived in in a pretty ghetto apartment complex a few miles away from school. One night we were sitting on the couch watching television when we heard four very loud noises in a

[3]Genesis 1:26.

row. I knew immediately what they were. I had just heard gunshots not too far from our apartment building. Grace looked at me and said in a somewhat startled but somewhat I – knew – this – would – happen – because – of – where – we – live type of look and said, "What was that?" "Oh, probably nothing," I said back to her. "I think someone is just hammering something into the wall." She knew better though, and a few moments later we heard about ten cop cars come flying into our apartment complex. A young man had just been shot right outside our apartment door. It was a rather frightening evening for us.

A few weeks later I was sitting at my desk in our study working on a paper when I heard some nasty yelling coming from below my slightly cracked window. I looked outside to find a young girl being pinned down to her passenger side seat by a young man. This young man would not let this young girl get up. He had his two hands pinned to her shoulders and was screaming at her while she threw a fit in return. My heart immediately started pounding, and I got that horrible feeling in my stomach. I knew I had to go out there. In all honesty, I didn't want to at all. The guy looked really big from my little window, and I was pretty out of shape at the time. And nobody in his or her right mind really likes conflict, especially the type of conflict that ensues out of the blue like that… and especially the type of conflict that could potentially leave you bloody.

I got up from my seat with my heart pounding and

headed for the door. My wife, Grace, had heard the yelling and screaming as well and she knew exactly where I was going as I headed out the door and down the stairs. She laughs as I retell this story to friends and loves to recount the fact that I spun around and said only this one sentence before I hurried out the door to save the day… "I might get shot."

I ran down the stairs to find that the guy had successfully crawled over the young girl's passenger side seat into the driver's side and was still holding her down as he attempted to drive the car away. I shouted what any young, brave, and nervous young man would say, "Guys, what's going on out here?" The man slammed on the breaks, opened the car door, and came right at me. I think I stopped breathing because this would have been the first "real" fight I had been involved in since middle school (me and my neighbors used to re-enact Fight Club in our back yards). Thankfully, the young man wasn't coming at me to fight. I think I startled him and he was pretty embarrassed. He came at me with high emotions trying to justify why he was acting the way he was, and the girl just ran toward me crying and hid behind my back.

I developed a little bit more courage and had the guy go stand on the other side of the street, as I made sure the young lady was safe inside her apartment complex before dealing with him. I walked her upstairs as she was crying hysterically and she immediately fell on the floor face first as she entered her apartment. My wife went into her apartment trying to console her, and I headed back downstairs to talk with the man who now was pacing frantically back and forth. I told him that he had two choices. He could either ride with me as I took him home, or I would call the police to come take him home. He chose the former, and we headed toward his home. I was still a little nervous though. This guy's emotions were running rather high, so I tried to change the topic of conversation to calm him down a bit and began to ask about his life. Little did I know he had just got out of jail that week after a few year stint and was heading over to see his ex-girlfriend, the mother of his child. I gripped the steering wheel a little tighter, said a silent prayer, and finally got him to his destination. I took him back to his house, headed back to mine, and arrived to see that my wife and the young lady who was being attacked were getting along just great.

I finally felt the fruit of preparing myself to be a protector. I don't tell this story to make me look like a big hero, I tell this story because I had no idea it was coming. Remember, I had been, and in many ways still am, preparing myself to be a protector. I had the joy of fulfilling this role rather tangibly that day. I didn't know what was going to come from the fact that I headed out that door with the attempt of stopping a young girl from being hurt by another man. He could have knocked my face in. He could potentially have shot me. There are many things that could have happened. And I'm rather grateful for the outcome that day. I pray that I face conflict like this with boldness in the future. I pray this prayer for you as well.

What's more, since the birth of my daughter, Cora, the concept of protection has become even more of a heightened reality. The concepts of provision and protection really become a reality when you become father.

How Should We Protect Women?

THERE ARE MANY ways in which men should fulfill this role. First, the aforementioned discussion and immediate context of this word points to physical protection. We have discussed this in detail. As men, we are to physically protect women and children *from all danger*.

Second, we are to protect them *emotionally*. This is more specific to a boyfriend and girlfriend type of relationship. If you are a young guy in a dating relationship then I urge you to begin to think through this concept with me. I didn't tell Grace that I loved her until I was on one knee with a ring in my hand. I let her know from the beginning of our relationship that I was going to do my best to protect her emotions from being attached to me completely without any form of tangible commitment (i.e., an engagement ring). This was my way of going about protecting her in this way. Maybe it is different for you, but I would strongly advise against flippantly throwing around the phrase, "I love you," without any form of commitment attached to it. Contrary to popular western-culture belief, love is not an emotion. Love should always come with a commitment. As men, we should always walk with this kind of urgency toward our commitments. Let us not be a wave of the sea blown and tossed by the wind. Show your manhood to her not by playing with her emotions but by protecting them.

Third, we are to protect them *sexually*. This is also specific to a boyfriend and girlfriend type of relationship, as well as any relationship outside of the marriage.[4] With the overdose of sex in our culture, it seems like the quest for holiness is more difficult than ever. We must battle for holiness in everything that we do. If pornography is gripping our hearts then we must cut it off from our lives. Get rid of your computer. Put safe guards on your Internet.[5] But above all, take captive your thoughts to Jesus. For it is in him we find sanctuary from the lusts of our flesh. Let us fight for holiness. Let us be men who protect women sexually.

How Do I Practice This in My Own Marriage?

FINALLY, I WOULD like to provide you with tangible ways that I practice the calling of being a protector as a man and as a husband. This list is absolutely not ex-

[4]Matthew 15:19; Mark 7:21; Acts 15:20; 15:29; 21:25; Romans 1:24; 1:26; 7:3; 13:3; 1 Corinthians 5:1; 5:9; 5:11; 6:9; 6:12; 6:13; 6:18; 7:1; 7:2; 10:8; 12:21; Galatians 5:19; Ephesians 5:3; Colossians 3:5; 1 Thessalonians 4:3; 1 Timothy 1:10; Hebrews 12:16; 13:4; Jude 1:7; Revelation 2:14; 2:20; 9:21; 21:8: 22:15.

[5]Covenant Eyes and XXX Church are both great sites for this.

haustive, although I promise you that I do practice them daily, and I can also promise you that I still fail at them often. By God's grace, I am *learning* to be a man who practices this reformational approach to manhood. I pray that this list encourages you to think intentionally about your day-to-day calling as a protector, and I pray that you find many more creative ways to practice protecting women and children appropriate to your differing relationships with them.

- I always try to be aware of my surroundings, no matter where we are.
- I always sit facing the front door in restaurants.
- I always open every door for Grace.
- I always walk on the inside of the sidewalk to protect her from the coming traffic.
- I always drive, if available.
- I always get out to pump gas.
- I always take the dog out at night, or run to the car at night, or do anything outside at night for her.
- I always make sure the house is locked up.
- I am always the first one to go into the house.
- I always make sure Grace is comfortable with *and* in her surroundings.

In him we have obtained an inheritance, having been predestined according to the purpose of him who works all things according to the counsel of his will. PAUL, *Ephesians 1:11*

—CHAPTER EIGHT—

†

FRIENDLY FIRE

Learning to Make Quick Decisions Amidst Numerous Responsibilities

MAKING GOOD DECISIONS is hard work.

I have made so many bad decisions in my life that I could honestly turn the bad decisions of my life into a book. I have made poor decisions that have led to sin, and I have made many poor decisions, while not necessarily leading to sin, that have still been quite poor decisions. Nonetheless, I do not want to bask in my mistakes and glorify any poor decision that I have made that might have led me into sin. What I do want to do, however, is affirm our ability, as men, to make good and wise decisions. I want to ask and attempt to answer the following questions in this chapter:

- How do the decisions I make fall under the umbrella of God's sovereignty? (A Good Theology of Decision Making)

- Does God have a specific plan for my life? (God's Plan & Our Obedience)
- How does God speak to us and lead us in making decisions? (God Speaks, We *Read*)
- How do I make a good decision? (A Route for Making Wise Decisions)

The ability to make good and quick decisions is something that might not fall directly under the umbrella of what a man is supposed to be, but I am absolutely convinced that this is a trait good leaders, and men in general, must possess. Consider this more of a small umbrella under the bigger umbrella of what reformational manhood is all about. We have watered down the ability to make wise and informed decisions in the church today. We use the so-called "God Card" to avoid hard decisions we don't want to make or conversations that we don't want to have. We also use the "God Card" often times to avoid the truth. For instance, how many times have you gotten yourself out of something, whether it is a commitment, a relationship, etc., by using the "God Card?" You might say, "Oh, I'm just not feeling like God wants me to be here." Or, "Oh, I just don't feel like God wants us to be together." Or using it the opposite way, "God told us to be together." Kevin DeYoung, in his book, *Just Do*

Something,[1] humorously states how funny it is when folks say something to this affect. If this is the case and God did tell you this interesting news then why didn't he tell the other person as well?

- Please don't ever use the "God Card." A man should never speak like this.
- Also, a man should hold to his commitments, end relationships truthfully, and lead well.
- A good leader is a good and quick decision-maker amidst numerous possibilities.

We've all been there before; making quick decisions amidst numerous possibilities sometimes seems rather impossible. We can choose A or B or C or, sometimes, even D. This is what is known as opportunity cost. When we choose opportunity A, we forfeit the route of opportunities B, C, and D. This is not just the case with big decisions like *Should I move to Texas? Should I marry this girl? Should I go to this college?* or *Should I pursue this degree?* This is simply the case for every decision we make in life. Every ostensibly smaller decision we make is also bound by this concept of opportunity cost. As men, this is where we find our "what we're made of" moments. What we are made of as men is evident in how we make decisions.

Before I go any further I do want to say something about our responsibility to make decisions as it is found under the umbrella of God's sovereignty. God is

[1]Kevin Deyoung, *Just Do Something: How to Make A Decision Without Dreams, Visions, Fleeces, Impressions, Open Doors, Random Bible Verses, Casting Lots, Liver Shivers, Writing in the Sky, Etc.* (Chicago, IL: Moody Publishers, 2009).

completely sovereign. He is King. He knows everything. Every decision we make falls under his sovereign direction. Yet we still have the responsibility to make well-in-formed and wise decisions. So, with that said, let us ask the question, "What is God's role in our decision making?"

A Good Theology of Making Decisions

LET US BEGIN with God.

God created everything (Gen. 1, Heb. 11:3). He has communicable attributes (attributes God shares) and incommunicable attributes (attributes that God does not share). Examples of God's communicable attributes are love, knowledge, mercy, justice, and grace. Examples of God's incommunicable attributes are God's unchangeableness, eternity, and omnipresence. The picture here that I want to paint for you is that God is both infinite and personal. He has existed before and outside of time, albeit he still has created us for his glory and desires for us to live in relationship with him and with each other for our good.

He created humanity and we are his image-bearers (Gen 1:27). Man then fell into sin (Gen. 3), and this screwed up our ability to make *good* decisions.

You see, before the fall, Adam and Eve had really only one major decision—the decision to obey God. They lived in perfect harmony with one another and with God. They were called to cultivate the Garden, subdue it, reproduce and multiply, and obey God.

Early in the story, we see they had many other decisions as well. Adam was to make the decision on what to name each animal and what to name Eve. These were big decisions. We are then presented with Adam and Eve's decision when faced with the temptation of eating the fruit. They were not supposed to eat the fruit. This was the first bad decision recorded in all of Scripture. In fact, it was so bad that it fractured the entire created order and thus sin was born into human existence.

From then on, humanity has made many bad decisions. Our existence has been plagued with poor decisions. Some decisions have been so bad that they have attempted to wipe out entire villages, cities, and even people groups. Think Hitler, Stalin, and Mussolini.

We, as sinners, make bad decisions all the time. Maybe not on a Hitler—scale, but we make bad decisions every day. Some of these decisions lead to sin. Others might just be stupid. But what about our ability to make decisions under the umbrella of God's sovereignty? It should be no secret by now that I am a strong advocate for the sovereignty of God. Maybe it could be stated like this: God in his sovereignty has elected and predestined us to be saved; therefore, we must act like men according to his Word and will. Nonetheless, one of the most amazing things about God's character and attributes in comparison to our finiteness and sinfulness is that it points to a beautiful paradox. God is sovereign, yet we are still called to be obedient to him, and part of this obedience is the ability to make good decisions. These good decisions can point us away from temptation or sin or they can be game changers that will affect the rest of our lives as we know it. Choosing opportunity A will not allow us to choose B, C, or D. So, how do we reckon this? For starters, let us remember that God always gets his way.

Kevin DeYoung gives a great synopsis of God's will of decree and will of desire. He rightly says,

> If we examine the Bible, we see that God's will has two sides to it. On the first side is God's *will of decree*. This refers to what God has ordained. Everything that comes to pass is according to God's sovereign decree. And all that He decrees will ultimately come to pass. God's will of decree cannot be thwarted. It is immutable and fixed.[2]

God's will of decree should be viewed in great light. What God wills to happen, in fact, will happen. As men, we must be able to not only understand this truth, but also be able to live well within its reality. God is sovereign over all things. This should give us great comfort.

He continues…

> The other side of the coin is God's *will of desire*. This refers to what God has commanded—what

---

[2]DeYoung, Kevin, *Just Do Something: A Liberating Approach to Finding God's Will, or, how to make a decision without dreams, visions, fleeces, impressions, open doors, random bible verses, casting lots, liver shivers, writing in the sky, etc.*, (Chicago: Moody Publishers, 2009), 19.

He desires from His creatures. If the will of decree is how things are, the will of desire is how things ought to be.[3]

You may have now realized that we have a massive dilemma on our hands. The question of God's sovereignty and human responsibility is a big one. How can God decree everything, but still hold us accountable for our actions as humans? Though this concept might give us headaches when we dive into it, the Bible clearly affirms both of these things. The Bible teaches us that God is sovereign, but he is not the author of sin. As humans, we live under his sovereignty, but are not free from the responsibility of our actions.[4]

So, we are left with a two-sided coin. On one side we have God's sovereignty and on the other we have human responsibility. On the human responsibility side we have the concept of being able to make good and wise decisions. As with DeYoung, there is no way I can do this theological conversation justice in this short little book, but a good place to look for guidance on this topic is Matthew 6:33, which says,

"But seek first the kingdom of God and his righteousness, and all these things will be added to you."

I believe it is here that we find our answer.

---

[3]Ibid., 22-23.

[4]God sent Babylon to punish Judah, but God also punished Babylon for acting wickedly against God's people (Jeremiah 25). Likewise, God planned the death of His Son and yet those who killed Christ were called lawless (Acts 2:23) – DeYoung, *Just Do Something*, 19.

God's Plan & Our Obedience

SCRIPTURE SPEAKS directly about God's plan for our lives. There are so many worthless resources out there about finding your best life now and how to figure out God's will for your life that we often forget that God's ultimate plan for our individual life is summed up in one phrase—growth in holiness.

> *Matthew 6:33: "But seek first the kingdom of God and his righteousness, and all these things will be added to you."*

We are to seek first God and his righteousness. This is God's plan for our lives. Everything else will be given to us if we are first seeking after God.

> *Ephesians 1:11: "In him we have obtained an inheritance, having been predestined according to the purpose of him who works all things according to the counsel of his will."*

Again, God always gets his way because he has caused everything to be so. When we seek his righteousness then it seems that everything will work according to his will. The only thing that does not conform to his will is sin.

> *Ephesians 2:10: "For we are his workmanship, created in Christ Jesus for good works, which God prepared beforehand, that we should walk in them."*

Not only will everything work out according to God's will, but also he has prepared his will for our lives before the foundations of the world. This should give us comfort when making the biggest of decisions. He has planned everything. He has numbered our steps. We are only called to be obedient and run after the kingdom of God. We are only called to chase after holiness and become more like Jesus. Everything else, according to God's sovereign will, has been prepared in advance. The jobs we'll have, the school we'll attend, the wife we'll choose... it has all been prepared in advance.

God Speaks, We *Read*

I HAVE BEEN told so many times by well-intentioned people that God is speaking to them and telling them to do such and such a thing. This is using the "God Card" in reverse. God does not speak through dreams, visions, random bible verses, arbitrary situations, or the casting of lots. Well, he did work through a few of these mediums in the Bible, but he does not work this way anymore. In the Old Testament, God spoke to his people in several different ways. Mainly, he spoke to them through the prophets. He would directly speak to a prophet and the prophet would then speak God's Words to Israel. He would also direct people to decisions by the casting of lots. Lots were used in the Old Testament to make decisions and understand God's directing will.

In the New Testament, God still spoke to the apostles directly in the writing of Scripture through the avenue of the Holy Spirit, but more specifically God spoke to them through Jesus. Hebrews 1:1-2 says,

> *"Long ago, at many times and in many ways, God spoke to our fathers by the prophets, but in these last days he has spoken to us by his Son, whom he appointed the heir of all things, through whom also he created the world."*

Today, God speaks to us through the direct revelation of his son in Scripture.

Simply put: God speaks, we read.

And we read about Jesus in God's Word through the Holy Spirit who indwells inside of us.

We do see the disciples cast lots to pick the disciple who would follow Jesus in Acts 1, but we must understand that that was before the sending of the Holy Spirit. The Spirit was sent in Acts 2. We don't cast lots today because we have the Holy Spirit. We don't choose random Bible verses today because we have the Holy Spirit. We don't make decisions through dreams and visions because, again, we have the Holy Spirit. But we don't just rely on the Holy Spirit without Scripture to guide us in decision making. Yes, he is an instrumental part of the process, but God has also given us many helps in making well-advised, quick, and biblically rich decisions.

A Route for Making Wise Decisions

WITH ALL OF this said, I want to give you a route for making big, quick, and wise decisions.

As men we must begin to cultivate the ability to make good decisions that have long-term effects rather quickly. As leaders we must have the ability to do this well. Leaders often make decisions on the fly, in the heat of the moment, and each decision is expected to be beneficial for the good of the organization.

Here are some personal rules that I use for making big decisions:

1. Pray about it.

I MAKE SURE that every BIG decision is always taken before the Lord in a humble manner. I pray that God would reveal his will to me through his Scripture, through wise counsel, and through the ability to make a wise decision.

2. What does Scripture say?

I ALWAYS ASK this question second. What does the Bible say about this issue? Make sure to avoid proof texting here or choosing a random Bible verse. We must interpret Scripture with Scripture, and we must look at a topic from Genesis to Revelation to see what the entire counsel of God's Word says about it. The next step is crucial every time and is especially beneficial when dealing with issues the Bible does not directly address.

3. Seek wise counsel.

ASK THE ADVICE of those in your life that are wise. Make sure to ask those who won't just tell you what you want to hear. Remember, there is wisdom in a multitude of counselors (Proverbs 11:14), and that is what we are all about here… making decisions with wisdom.

4. What are your desires?

MANY PEOPLE often downplay this last point, but I want to highlight this last point as the icing on the cake when making decisions. Desires, if righteous, are God given. We must not turn away from our desires as mystical or play off our desire with the thought of God's will not being our own. Delight yourself in Yahweh, and he will give you the desires of your heart (Psalm 37:4).

Finally, we must always remember that the chief end of man is to glorify God and enjoy him forever (*Westminster Shorter Catechism*, letter A). Whatever we decide to do with our life must be seen under the umbrella of this glorious truth. When we understand this truth, we might not know exactly what God wants us to do regarding a major or a career, but we will know what the entire aim of our life is and always will be with absolute certainty.

As for me, and with everything I have put forth in

this book, I am still learning to master these traits. Something tells me that I won't ever master them fully. I am learning every day to lead my family well by working with my wife to make wise decisions. I am learning every day to make wise decisions on the fly or in the heat of the moment. I am learning every day to make wise decisions that will affect the people that I lead.

Remember, we don't want to be wishy-washy decision-makers and use the Holy Spirit like he is some sort of fairy tale character speaking directly to us. I never trust those types of guys. Let us be men who make well-informed, quick, and wise decisions for the glory of God and the benefit of our families, churches, and leadership platforms.

And just a few words about how to think, act, and feel *after* a decision is made.

Once a decision is made: 1) Go with it. Don't waffle just because you're unsure. If it proves to be a bad decision, and you can turn from it, then turn from it. Otherwise, go with it. 2) This is connected with the first point—accept the consequences of your decisions one way or the other. This doesn't mean brushing off repercussions, it means taking them seriously, but taking them for yourself. If *you* made the decision, then *you* take the responsibility for the consequences, whether it is disaster or great reward. "Taking it like a man" means not letting those under your leadership take the heat you should bear. If you have people under you, your leadership becomes valuable to them when it protects them from negative consequences. That's why the high-school employee always gets his manager when a customer is angry. The manager is protecting his employees by saying "This is my responsibility." And err on the side of taking more responsibility rather than less. You can even selflessly lead by taking more than your share. And don't tell a soul. 3) Trust God and be at peace. Trust that he is sovereign over your life, and may have something in store for you other than what you can see or imagine for yourself. And trust that God's love is *redeeming*, turning even your bad and sinful decisions for good.

And when we fail, as we will soon enough, let us repent quickly, learn from our poor decisions, and teach others not to make the same ones. As time moves away from that stupid decision we made, let us learn to teach others not to do the same. And ultimately, let us rest in his glorious sovereignty. For there we will find our strength.

So, whether you eat or drink, or whatever you do, do all to the glory of God.
PAUL, *1 Corinthians 10:31*

—CHAPTER NINE—

R & R

Learning to Redeem My Time from Brainless & Stupid Activities

LIKE MUCH OF my journey into manhood, I have learned this specific trait over time, from experience, and from those around me, while still continuing to learn and apply what I am learning every single day. God has been continually teaching me a ton about how to use my time for his glory. I pray these examples serve you well.

When I was in high school I spent the majority of my waking time playing basketball. All of my priorities and all of my thought life were geared toward the game of basketball. It was my god. It was my idol. While growing up and playing basketball, I also watched my dad work hard and have specific priorities that really set the tone for how our family was going to function. He worked hard at his job. He worked hard as a father.

He worked hard as a husband. He always had my brother and me in church. Growing up, I knew what to expect out of my dad. This type of work ethic and decision making, especially as it leads to how I structure my priorities, has soaked into me over the years.

I worked extremely hard on the basketball court, creating opportunities for myself that most six foot one inch white guys don't really have. I had the opportunity to play for an AAU traveling team that produced five division-one players and one NBA star. Because of my hard work, I was well known throughout Knoxville for my basketball ability. I probably wasn't the best in the city but I was up there.

I brought this work ethic to college. I played college basketball for a semester, but God was beginning to mold my life and my calling outside of basketball and into the local church. At the time, I had zero idea of where that specific calling would take me. As I have previously mentioned, I went to Boyce College in Louisville, Kentucky to pursue pastoral training, and was surrounded there by some great leaders. It was there that I learned more about having a Jesus-centered and redemptive perspective on my time and priorities than anywhere else. I watched men be successful pastors, professors, husbands, fathers, writers, and preachers, all within the confines of a 24-hour day. I found myself wanting to be like these men!

A funny, yet somewhat crude, joke that went around campus that was probably fashioned by simply observing the lifestyles of these great men was, "If you have too much time on your hands, then you probably have too much 'time' on your hands." Time being a euphemism for masturbation. Therefore, this perspective was continually drilled in me.

Not only do I want to use my time well and order my priorities appropriately, but I want to structure my time in such a way that I will not fall into sin because of laziness and sloth.

Over the past couple of years, I have learned that God has allowed me to put a lot on my plate and still manage to function like a sane person. I don't know if it is my personality that allows me to function in this way, or if it is simply a learned trait, or maybe both, but I have the ability to do lots of things at one time. Other people have affirmed this in my life as well. My last two semesters in seminary, I took a total of 18 hours each. That is literally two semesters in one. During those two semesters I was able to accomplish two full years of school, graduating from seminary in a total of three years. I could have finished in two and a half years but during one semester I only took six hours because I was newly married and working about 60 hours a week.

During this time, I was working full-time as a pastor and directing a ministry that I had recently founded called *The Veritas Network*, which took about 15-20 hours more a week at the time. Combine all of these responsibilities with being a husband and soon-to-be-father and I was swamped. I struggled to keep my head above water at times. I was so overwhelmed each day with tasks that I needed to get done that I found myself neglecting my responsibilities as a husband and even as a follower of Jesus Christ. Since then, God has graciously allowed me to restructure my priorities accordingly, bring other people around me who can accomplish these tasks each day, rest in their ability to do these tasks well, refocus on what is really important, and simply have time for my family, church, and other priorities that are and should have been higher than paper pushing and marking things off lists.

The purpose of this chapter is to encourage young guys to begin to think about how they are structuring their priorities. I have watched so many young people spend hours a day in front of the video game console that they cannot be structuring their priorities and time in a redemptive manner. I pray that you would begin to think through how you are structuring your priorities now. Do you have too much time on your hands?

Redeeming the Time...On Your Hands

I LOVE ENTERTAINMENT. I'll be the first to admit it. I love going to see movies, spending time with friends and family around a television set watching sports, and hanging out with my wife as we work through all 8 seasons of the show 24. I love it! I have grown up in a culture that is centered on entertainment. I grew up playing video games. Growing up, I had almost every single video game console there was. What is more, I love surfing the Internet. I love spending time surfing web pages, updating social network statuses, and just hanging out at good sites. I love being entertained. I love sitting on the couch and making my brain go numb as I watch something brainless. And as a man, I have had to learn to fight against these tendencies for the past couple of years.

Our culture suggests that we men waste most of our time. We play video games. We watch hours and hours of television. And we spend hours a week, sometimes hours a day, watching movies or surfing the Internet. Brainless and stupid activities have become the backbone of who we are, especially as men. Our culture is centered upon the rise of entertainment. We pay athletes, movie stars, and other celebrities millions and millions of dollars for the entertainment they provide to us.

In 2005, the Times Online in London, England reported that a 28-year-old man literally dropped dead from playing 50 hours of games straight.[1] He had so much entertainment that it killed him. Too much of a good thing is never a good thing.

A multi-billion dollar company that didn't exist in our vocabulary ten years ago has changed the way we spend our time. Facebook began around 2004. According to its own website, it has more than 500 million users. 50% of its active users log on to Facebook

---

[1]http://www.timesonline.co.uk/tol/news/world/article553840.ece

every single day. An average user has around 130 friends. And get this: average users stay on Facebook for over 55+ minutes a day. That is at least 9,470 minutes a year, 324 hours a year, and 13+ days a year that the average user spends on Facebook. People spend a total of over 700 billion minutes per month on Facebook. That is a lot of wasted minutes.

That is a lot of time spending our time doing nothing, or what I like to call brainless activities.

Then we calculate all the television we watch, Internet surfing that we do, and movies we consume, and we probably spend a good majority of our waking hours being entertained by brainless activities. The average American spends four or more hours in front of a television per day. That is nuts. And some days I ashamedly fall within that category, especially if the Final Four basketball tournament is on that day.

As Christians we must intentionally think through how we are spending our time, especially as Christian men. We are called to be leaders, providers, and protectors. We are to do all these things *before* we sit down for our brainless activities. I heard a preacher whom I respect greatly say once that our jobs don't end at 5:00 PM. As husbands and fathers, our jobs end when the rest of the family goes to bed. So, when does that leave time for brainless activities like the ones mentioned above?

The Apostle Paul writes to the church in Corinth urging them to use their time and activities for the glory of God (1 Cor. 10:31). He exhorts us to eat, drink, and do everything for his glory. This is no small task. As men, we eat and drink. And as men, we have wives, kids, local church priorities, jobs, hobbies, daily tasks, family vacations, gym memberships, friendships, and countless other monthly, weekly, and even daily activities that hang in front of us. James urges us to not waste our life because our lives are simply vapor that appear for a little while but then vanish (Jas 4:14). When we take all of this, all of our daily responsibilities we are called to as men, combined with the daily tasks we choose to do, how can we find the time for such brainless activities?

Now before I sound like a banging symbol, allow me to provide a few prefatory remarks.

Entertainment is not a bad thing. I love it. I have a wife who doesn't like it as much as I do, so it is easier for me to balance my entertainment consumption at times. Solomon, in all of his great wisdom, tells us that there is a time for everything (Ecc. 3:1-15). There is a time to be born and a time to die, a time to laugh, a time to cry, a time to speak, a time to work, a time to eat and drink, and a time for brainless activities (i.e., television, movies, Internet, etc.).

I have learned over the course of the last few years a good rule of thumb that I would like to pass on to you: entertainment is a good thing when everything else you need to do has been completed.

When I sit in front of the television at night, I sit in front of it knowing that all my tasks and duties as a man for the day have been completed. Maybe there are a few times that I haven't finished everything I needed to do that day, but I try for the most part to do what needs to be done first, and then enjoy a time of rest and relaxation.

This is what is called redeeming the time.

Redeeming the time allows you to view your time as valuable. It allows you to view your time in light of eternity and in light of your responsibilities as a man. Redeeming the time allows you to have a perspective that is specifically Christ-centered. When you do this then you view your time and priorities in a redemptive light. So, let me ask you, how do you need to begin to redeem your time from brainless and stupid activities?

Because I am task-orientated and have an extremely high A-type personality, I wake up every morning and make a list of everything I need to do that day. I call it an A-List. Many times, I am simply carrying my list over from the previous day. I go to bed knowing exactly what I need to do the next day. I often go about my day overly task oriented, marking things off my list one at a time, many times at the expense of caring for people. We must be men who redeem the time and order our priorities rightly.

Our Top Priorities as Christ Followers

HERE IS WHAT I would submit to you a follower of Jesus Christ's priorities should in fact be:

1. Your relationship with Jesus.

THIS IS NUMBER one. This is the highest priority in life. This is our ultimate aim and our ultimate goal. How are you doing in this area? Are you spending a sufficient amount of time with Jesus each day? The amount of time we spend with Christ each day borders on being relative to each person and each person's schedule; however, we should always focus on planning out time each day to read Scripture, spend time in prayer, and get away from all the busyness that life brings and just sit and focus on the gospel of Jesus Christ. When was the last time you spent a good amount time with your Savior? When was the last time you were on your knees in your bedroom? Do you need to reprioritize your schedule so that you can spend more time with Christ? If so, wake up an extra 30 minutes earlier each day, put down the PlayStation controller, turn off the television, close down the computer, and go spend time with your Maker.

2. Your position as a husband.

MAYBE YOU ARE not to this point yet. Maybe you are only a teenager at this point in your life. Maybe you are an older man, beyond your teenage years, yet still single. If this is you then I would encourage you to continue to make this pursuit a top priority. As men we are called to leave our father and mother's house and hold fast to our wife (Genesis 2). If you are indeed older and you haven't found yourself yet attempting to pursue this glorious pursuit of being a husband then I would absolutely encourage you to do so. There is nothing greater than finding a spouse to share life with.

To all the married folks reading this book, this is our second highest priority outside of our relationship with Jesus. The majority of our attention should be placed upon our spouses above everything else. This should be a top priority to us as men. If we are neglecting this area of leadership than we must, with urgency, reevaluate our life and restructure our priorities and begin to place our wives at the top of the list.

3. Your position as a father.

BEHIND YOUR relationship with Jesus and your position as a husband, you should be focused on the pursuit of being the best father you can possibly be. Again, if those of you reading this book are not to this point then I pray that you would begin to become passionate about this pursuit. First, find a wife; second, begin a family. There is nothing more beautiful than seeing two people come together and begin a family with the gospel of Jesus Christ as its center.

Men, we should be focused on becoming the best father's we absolutely know how to be. Begin to read books on parenting. Listen to sermons on parenting. Go to parenting conferences. Get around men whom you have identified as really good fathers. Ask them questions. Learn from them. Repent of your mistakes. Strive forward wanting to learn. Strive forward wanting to be the best father you can possibly be for the glory of God alone. One thing is for certain, as parents we are called to be the primary disciple-makers of our children. It is a common misconception that the youth pastor is the primary disciple-maker of young people. This is absolutely not the case. Parents must disciple their own children. Fathers, you will one day stand before God and give an account of how you led your family. May we be prepared to unravel very detail on how we attempted to lead our families well!

4. Your involvement in the local church.

THIS IS MORE than just going and sitting on Sunday mornings. This means getting involved in the ministries of your local church. It means being committed to serving in your local church. Get involved in a small group or a Bible study. Become committed to growing as a disciple of Jesus Christ. We often place so many other things above our commitment to the local church that we find ourselves not really involved in the life of the church at all. Get plugged in. Start serving. Get committed. Start giving. Make this a top priority.

5. Your work or school.

I WOULD SUBMIT to you that your priority of working, your job, or your career should be way down the list.

Yes, we should absolutely work. I am a firm believer that men should work and work hard for that matter. But when we place our careers above our relationship with Jesus, above our families, and above our involvement in our local church then we really need to reevaluate our priorities. Often times, as men, our jobs become our lives. This is especially the case for task-oriented people like me. I heard a great little quote that is extremely simple, yet pertinent to this discussion. It goes like this: "You have your job, and then you have your life." How much more simple can it get? Men, we have our work. We have our jobs. We have our means for providing for our families. But then we have our life! May we be men who prioritize our lives in this way. May we be men who are so passionate about leading our families and leading in the local church that our ""work" ends when we walk into the door of our homes.

Young guys, let us not put school above our involvement with our local church either. Remember, loving Jesus cannot be separated from loving the church because Jesus came to die for the church and give his life for the church. I have seen so many young people not get involved with the life of the church because they simply have a million and one things going on in their lives. They have extracurricular activities. They have other activities. They have expectations given to them by their parents. They have sports. They have friends. They have a social life. Only *after* all these things do they participate in the life of the local church. May this be a generation that is committed to the life of the church, to loving the church, and serving in the local church.

6. Your fun.

OFTEN TIMES we put our fun as a top priority, when in fact we should absolutely partake in fun, but *only after* we have completed our previous priorities. Ironically, as I write this chapter, I find myself on a plane flying out to Colorado with my wife to play in the backcountry of the Rocky Mountains for the next week or so. This is not usually how our fun times work though. This specific vacation was a long time coming. What's more, we have to plan out our fun times at the Gibson household. I am so task-oriented and list-driven that we often times have to plan out our fun each week. I can get so caught up in priorities 4 and 5 (church stuff and work stuff) that I neglect priorities 1) my relationship with Jesus; 2) my position as a husband; and even 6) having a good time now and again. I get emails from Grace throughout the day reminding me that we have scheduled fun-time that night. FUN-TIME means no phone, no computer, no Internet, no work—just fun! We call these fun times Thursday Night Date Nights. Our current circumstances allow us to go on a date each week. It is absolutely the best part of my week! I am so thankful for the good times that my wife and I have together.

If your abundant lifestyles are causing you to have these priorities out of order than you need to reevaluate your lifestyles. If you are working more than being involved in the local church because you can't keep up with the lifestyle you want to live, than it is your obligation as a follower of Christ to change your lifestyle.

In short, your priorities should always be structured this way—God, Family, Church, Work, and Fun.

In saying all of this, I pray that you would see that becoming a Jesus-like and gospel-centered man is not another law or commandment that is given to us on top of the two greatest commandments. If we love God and love others than we will do well at striving to be this type of man. But when we fail, and we will all fail at times, let us always look to Jesus, the perfect man, who satisfied all of our failures and sins on the cross.

May we be a generation who gets off the couch, puts the game controllers down, shuts down the computer, and turns off the television… at least until all of our other priorities and responsibilities have been completed. And may we be a generation marked with repentance when we find ourselves with 'too much time on our hands.'

"I am the way, the truth, and the life, no one comes to the Father except through me."
JESUS, *John 14:6*

—CHAPTER TEN—

JESUS
The Only Perfect Man

IT HAS BEEN MY most important task and mission to make much of Jesus throughout this book. It is not about you. It is all about him. In reality, as we pursue manhood as defined in this book, we are not simply trying to conform to a set of ideals or to a moral framework alien to Scripture. Rather, we are conforming ourselves to the person of Jesus Christ, our Savior and King. We are becoming more like him. We are becoming better men who are like him. We are becoming better husbands who are like him. We are becoming better fathers who are like him. We are becoming better sons who are like him. We are becoming better brothers who are like him. We are becoming better leaders who are like him. We are becoming better providers who are like him. We are becoming better protectors who are like him. We are becoming better decision makers who are like him. We are becoming better defenders of truth who are like him. We are becoming more like him in every way!

We must realize though that we will never be fully like Jesus. Well, not until we either die and become like him in our glorified state or until he comes back, whichever happens first. Sanctification is a process. It is a process of becoming more like him. It is a process of defeating sin in our lives and clothing ourselves with holiness. Reformational manhood is a process—a process of growing, learning, applying, evaluating, and of continually becoming more like him. It is a process of identifying where we suck as men, repenting of those sins, killing those sins, and running after Jesus. And when we fall back into those sins, it is the process of repentance all over again. May we be slow to anger but quick to repentance!

I want to remind you of how we defined the gospel in Chapter Three:

The gospel is the message that God, the Father, created the world good, and created humans in his image as very good. Man was created to be in relationship with his Creator and to give glory to him in all things, but early in the story man sinned by substituting himself for God and in so doing all of creation was affected. Sin in turn separated man from God. The rest of the story finds man in turmoil with God and in need of a Savior to pay the punishment for sin that man deserves. Man could not pay his own debt. Jesus, God the Son, then came to earth and lived a perfect life—because we could not—and died on a cross as a substitute for sin. In doing so, Jesus substituted himself for us, taking the punishment that we deserve—in the same way Adam substituted himself for God in the garden. Jesus arose from the dead, defeating death and ascended into Heaven at the Father's right hand. After taking his rightful place, Jesus sent God, the Holy Spirit, to call people to salvation, redeem cities and cultures, and build his church until he comes back. He is making all things new. Jesus, through the Spirit, is calling everybody everywhere to repent of all sin and to put their faith in him for the forgiveness of sin. Jesus will return, but he will not return empty handed. He will bring the New Heavens and New Earth. He will return as a Warrior King—one who completely defeats sin and death and ushers in the completeness of *shalom* (peace). He will then judge all people everywhere who have ever lived on earth, whether or not they have repented of sin and have put their faith in him. Jesus will then judge everybody who has ever lived. He will then graciously forgive those who do repent and punish those who do not by sending them to the real, eternal, and conscience torments of hell.

What a warrior-like hope! What a warrior-like reality that we actually find ourselves within! As men, we are going into battle everyday with the message of gospel as our sword. May we preach it to ourselves constantly, as he is the one we are trying to become like.

With that in mind, let us discuss why Jesus is in fact

central to this approach to biblical manhood.

1. Jesus would have never painted his toenails.

CONTRARY TO THE pictures and paintings that make Jesus out to be a wimpy man who has long flowing feminine hair with googly eyes, Jesus was a warrior. Yes, he was a gentle warrior. He did not come to bring a political revolution but a Kingdom through peaceful, albeit brutal methods. His method was his own crucifixion and death. He was a warrior who took on sin and death and was triumphant over them both.

What is more, Jesus would have never blurred the lines of what it meant to be completely masculine, as opposed to being completely feminine. God, the Father, created all things through Jesus Christ. He created them good, as they were intended to be. He created men and women in his image. He created men to be purely masculine. He created women to be purely feminine. Adam then substituted himself for God and fractured all things. Nothing was as it was intended to be anymore. The gospel, however, changes all of that. As the gospel goes forth, creation is renewed, perspectives become new, worldviews become new, and approaches to manhood become new.

As stated in Chapter One, I realize that toenail polish is completely a cultural thing. In the western culture, it is marked as a feminine thing. Therefore, we must distinguish ourselves according to our culture. We must distinguish ourselves as men. We must distinguish ourselves as women. In understanding culture and gender roles in this way, we come to the conclusion that Jesus would have never blurred the lines and clothed himself in feminine ways according to his culture. He was the most masculine man ever to live. He was what men were intended to be in the Garden of Eden before sin entered into the world. And he is what men will become in our glorified state. Until then, let us strive to be like him in all things.

2. Jesus was the most courageous man to ever live.

JESUS, LIKE NO man who has ever lived, willingly sacrificed his life for all of humanity. With courage he took the cross, died for sin, and defeated it. He is our example of courage, whether it is physical courage, moral courage, mental courage, etc. For now on, when we think of courageous men let us put Jesus Christ above the mental picture of William Wallace in our minds.

3. Jesus was the greatest defender of truth to ever live.

AS QUOTED AT THE beginning of this chapter, Jesus is the way, the truth, and the life. In a way, Jesus defended himself while he was on this earth. He was, and is, living, objective, and absolute truth to all of humanity.

He defended himself to religious leaders. He defended himself to his disciples. He defended himself in the temples. He defended himself in the city streets. He defended himself to his family. He defended himself at his trial. Jesus was living proof that truth exists in one absolute form.

As men who practice biblical manhood, we must defend Jesus in the same way that Jesus defended himself. We must defend truth with courage and boldness, not giving into the attacks of our culture. Christ is our King! Let us defend him boldly.

4. Jesus was the greatest proponent of marriage who ever lived.

ALTHOUGH JESUS was never married, he was the greatest proponent of marriage to ever live. He wasn't a proponent by example, of course, but by his living and teaching. Ephesians 5 is just one example. Christ served the church and gave himself up for her. In the same way a husband is to serve his wife like Christ served the church. Husbands are to serve their wives in this way, and wives are to love their husbands in this way. He gave us this picture of what marriage is all about by his life, ministry, death, and resurrection. Without Jesus, we have no basis for true biblical marriage. Without Jesus, we have no illustration of what true biblical marriage is all about.

5. Jesus was the greatest leader to ever live.

JESUS WAS THE greatest leader to ever walk this planet. He led by example. He led by being a servant leader. He led with authority. Everywhere he went people followed him. Thousands and thousands of people followed him. Today, millions, if not billions, of people claim to follow him. Jesus is the most influential and controversial man to ever live. He gave us a perfect example of what being a leader actually is.

6. Jesus was the greatest provider to ever live.

JESUS PROVIDED us with the greatest gift of all—merely himself. He didn't lavish us with material or perishable things. He did, however, lavish us with the greatest gift we could possibly receive. He gave us a way back to the Father. He provided for us salvation. He provided for us joy. He provided for us an eternity free from sin and death. He provided for us grace and mercy. All that we have to do is put our faith in him for the forgiveness of sin.

7. Jesus was the greatest protector to ever live.

DURING HIS EARTHLY ministry Jesus protected his followers from a life of sin, destruction, and eternal separation from God, the Father. Today, in much the same way, Jesus protects us by keeping us from lives of sin through God, the Holy Spirit. He is making us more like him, protecting us from our sinful natures, protecting our marriages, protecting our families, and protecting our churches. Jesus, through the Holy Spirit, is protecting us from losing our salvation. Once we are saved by grace through faith in Jesus, we are always in his grips.

8. Jesus was the greatest decision maker to ever live.

BECAUSE HE WAS the only perfect person to ever live on this planet, every decision he made was also perfect. He made perfect decisions for his family. He made perfect decisions for his disciples. He made perfect decisions at the time of his death. He made perfect decisions for the benefit of others. Today, through the Holy Spirit, Scripture, prayer, and other Godly people, Jesus helps us to make good and quick decisions for the benefit of others.

9. Jesus was the greatest redeemer of his time to ever live.

JESUS' TIME WAS always used to make much of the Father. Because he was fully human, we know that Jesus had a great sense of humor; he laughed and joked with the disciples, probably used wit in an unbelievable way, and had down time. However, Jesus never misused his time. He would have never played video games for hours and hours upon end. He would have never sat in front of a television for hours and hours upon end. Jesus used his time for the Kingdom. Today, Jesus is calling us to use our time to make much of the Father.

10. Jesus was the only perfect man to ever live.

AS WE HAVE SEEN, Jesus was absolutely perfect. He was flawless. He was without blemish. He was without error. Jesus was, in every single way, the most perfect man to ever live. As men, let us live like him, repenting along the way, applying what we learn, and pointing others toward him with our lives.

Though we ought not to take ourselves too seriously, we must take very seriously the opportunity to make much of Jesus.

—The Debrief—

†

Closing Remarks on Reformational Manhood

IN CHAPTER ONE, we defined biblical manhood as follows:

> A biblical man, marked with courage, is a leader, provider, and protector. He pursues his family, serves his church, shares and defends truth, makes good decisions, and redeems his time. And then teaches other men to do the same.

It has been my eager and passionate desire over the course of this book to explain to you this definition, talk with you about why we should be this type of man, and challenge you to apply its principles. This approach is defined specifically as a continual approach, a process of sanctification—ultimately, one that we will never fully achieve until Jesus takes us home and we become like him in our glorified state. A man is a leader. A man is a provider. A man is a protector of women and children according to his appropriate relationship with them. A man loves Jesus, his family, and the local church, in that order. A man is competent in defending truth and can articulate what the gospel of Jesus Christ is. A man has the ability to make quick and good decisions for the benefit of others. A man uses his time in a redemptive manner. A man strives for holiness above all things. What is more, it has been my purpose to explain this definition to you primarily from Scripture and secondly from my experience and journey into what a man is who practices this approach to biblical manhood.

Hopefully, I have approached this conversation humbly, yet sternly, displaying courage to talk about some not-so-popular views on manhood. And again, I pray that I have not come across cocky or egocentric. Sometimes passion and conviction can become confused with closed-mindedness and legalism. I hope that was not the case as you read these pages.

I pray that this book was extremely beneficial for you as you continue your journey into what a man who practices biblical manhood is. I pray that you would continue to pass this book along to others who might be thinking through this concept or who might need to read it for whatever reason. I pray that this book was useful for your sanctification, as you put sin to death, and strive to live a life worthy of the gospel of Jesus Christ. I pray that this book would spark an intentional, gospel-centered, and reformational manhood movement among this generation and the generations still to come.

I pray that this book would encourage older men to begin to teach younger men what biblical manhood is according to this approach, as it is defined in Titus 2. I pray that this book would bring you joy that is rooted in the pursuit of Jesus Christ alone. And, I pray that I would model this approach to biblical manhood in my life always. Still yet, I pray that I would repent quickly when I fail to do so. Ultimately, I pray that this book would bring glory to God, the Father, through Jesus Christ, as we continue to pursue and practice reformational manhood in our lives, in our marriages, in our families, and in our churches.

Thanks be to God for Jesus Christ, the perfect man.

Note from the Author

If I could be of any further assistance to you or you would like to dialogue with me in any way then please feel free to reach me at:

WEBSITE: http://ggblog.me
TWITTER: @gregrgibson

For Further Reading

The Abolition of Manhood

The Abolition of Man, C.S. Lewis

Physical, Moral, and Spiritual Courage

Crucial Confrontations: Never Walk Away from Another Conflict Again!, Kerry Patterson, Joseph Grenny, Ron McMillan, and Al Switzler,

Tempted and Tried: Temptations and the Triumph of Christ, Russell D. Moore

Knowing, Believing, and Defending the Gospel

He is There and He is Not Silent: Does it Make Sense to Believe in God?, Francis A Schaeffer

The Ever-Loving Truth: Can Faith Thrive in a Post-Christian Culture?, Vodie Baucham, JR.

The Gospel & Personal Evangelism, Mark Dever

Think: The Life of the Mind and the Love of God, John Piper

Total Truth: Liberating Christianity from Its Cultural Captivity, Nancy Pearcy

What is the Gospel?, Greg Gilbert

Marriage and Sexual Purity

God, Marriage, and Family: Rebuilding the Biblical Foundations, Andreas Kostenberger

Not Even a Hint: Guarding Your Heart Against Lust, Joshua Harris

Sex, Romance, and the Glory of God: What Every Christian Husband Needs to Know, C.J. Mahaney

The Exemplary Husband: A Biblical Perspective, Stuart Scott

Leadership, Provision, Protection

5 Levels of Leadership: Proven Steps to Maximize Your Potential, John C. Maxwell

Good to Great: Why Some Companies Make the Leap… and Others Don't, Jim Collins

Recovering Biblical Manhood and Womanhood: A Response to Evangelical Feminism, John Piper & Wayne Grudem

Spiritual Leadership: Principles of Excellence for Every Believer, J. Oswald Sanders

The 21 Irrefutable Laws of Leadership: Follow Them and People Will Follow You, John C. Maxwell

Decision Making

Just Do Something: A Liberating Approach to Finding God's Will, Kevin DeYoung

Redeeming Your Time

Amusing Ourselves to Death: Public Discourse in the Age of Show Business, Neil Postman

Spiritual Disciplines for the Christian Life, Donald Whitney

When I Don't Desire God: How to Fight for Joy, John Piper

Jesus

Vintage Jesus: Timeless Answers to Timely Questions, Mark Driscoll and Gerry Breshears

Scandalous: The Cross and Resurrection of Jesus, D.A. Carson

The Cross of Christ, John R. W. Stott

About the Author

Greg Gibson is the family pastor at Foothills Church in Maryville, TN. He received an M.Div. in biblical and theological studies from the Southern Baptist Theological Seminary, a B.A. in biblical studies from Boyce College, and is currently pursuing doctoral work. A contributing team member for the Council on Biblical Manhood & Womanhood, he is married to Grace and is the father of two children. Greg enjoys basketball and anything outdoors.

Reflections

Being Intentional about Manhood

What is one thing I can do today that will make me a better man?

____

____

____

What is something I can give up today that will make me a better man?

____

____

____

Why haven't I done this before?

____

____

____

____

____

What is something I am afraid of that a man should not be afraid of?

____

____

____

Write long-term goals involving fitness, diet, spiritual growth and personal courage.

If other people had to deal with me, would they be glad they did? If so why? If not why?

What is my greatest weakness and what can I do to change it?

Describe the man you want to be.

The ball is in your court now...

www.ingramcontent.com/pod-product-compliance
Lightning Source LLC
LaVergne TN
LVHW052024080426
835513LV00018B/2143